TWENTY-FIRST CENTURY
WARPLANES AND
HELICOPTERS

TWENTY-FIRST CENTURY
WARPLANES AND
HELICOPTERS

General Editor: Peter Darman

Grange BOOKS

This edition published in 2004 by Grange Books
Grange Books plc
The Grange
1–6 Kingsnorth Estate
Hoo
Near Rochester
Kent ME3 9ND
www.grangebooks.co.uk

© 2004 The Brown Reference Group plc

ISBN 1-84013-679-0

Printed in China

Editorial and design:
The Brown Reference Group plc
8 Chapel Place
Rivington Street
London
EC2A 3DQ
UK
www.brownreference.com

TWENTY-FIRST CENTURY
WARPLANES

CONTENTS

TWENTY-FIRST CENTURY MILITARY
HELICOPTERS

CONTENTS

AT-63 PAMPA

The Pampa is a single-engine, high-wing advance pilot trainer. Nineteen aircraft were originally built during the 1980s by Fabrica Militar de Aviones, the Argentine military depot that was privatized by the American company Lockheed Martin in 1995. Today there are 16 Pampas in service with the Argentine Air Force, which are deployed as part of the Air Training Command (the Argentinian Air Force consists of eight air brigades). The Pampas serve with *Escuadron de Caza 1*, which operates from Mendoza and El Plumerillo air bases. With a fully upgraded cockpit and modern avionics suite, the new AT-63 under production in Argentina is setting a new standard for a low-cost basic training aircraft, one which can also be used as an advanced trainer and light attack aircraft. The Argentine Air Force has contracted to build 12 AT-63s. On 19 June 2001, Lockheed Martin presented this new aircraft during the Paris Air Show and is now offering it to customers worldwide. The new generation AT-63 maintains the ease of maintenance and air-frame stability of the original version, produced in the late 1980s as the IA-63, while adding advanced upgrades and additional combat capabilities. The latest Pampa certainly ranks alongside the Hawk and Alpha as an effective trainer and light attack aircraft.

SPECIFICATIONS

Primary Role:	advanced trainer
Crew:	2
Contractor:	Lockheed Martin
Length:	10.9m (33.22ft)
Wingspan:	9.68m (31.75ft)
Height:	4.29m (14.1ft)
Maximum Take-off Weight:	3800kg (8377lb)
Powerplant:	1 x TFE-731-2C turbofan
Thrust:	1591kg (3500lb)
Maximum Speed:	750km/h (466mph)
Ceiling:	12,900m (42,323ft)
Range:	1500km (937 miles)
Armament:	1 x 30mm cannon pod
Systems:	1553B data bus, INS/GPS
Date Deployed:	2001

JH-7

This twin-engined, two-seat, swept-back, high-mounted wing supersonic fighter-bomber is designed to have the same role and configuration class as the Russian Sukhoi Su-24 Fencer. It has high mounted wings with compound sweepback and dog tooth leading edges; twin turbofans with lateral air intakes; all-swept tail surface, comprising large main fin, single small ventral fin and low set, all-moving tailplane; and a small overwing fence at approximately two-third span. Armament includes a twin-barrel 23mm gun in the nose, two stores pylons under each wing, plus a rail for close-range air-to-air missile (AAMs) at each wingtip. Typical underwing load for maritime attack includes two C-801 sea-skimming anti-ship missiles (ASMs) and two drop tanks. Though the JH-7 has provided the Chinese Navy with improved attack capabilities, the WS9 turbofan does not have enough thrust to equal foreign aircraft in the same weight class in terms of payload delivery. The Chinese plan is to use Russian-made engines and advanced composite materials to improve the aircraft and equip it with terrain-tracking radar and electronic countermeasures equipment. This improved JH-7A will have more reliable AL-31F engines and a radar with a detection range of 100km (62 miles) and the ability to simultaneously track 14 targets and attack 4 to 6.

SPECIFICATIONS

Primary Role:	fighter-bomber
Crew:	2
Contractor:	Xian Aircraft Industry Company
Length:	21m (68.89ft)
Wingspan:	12.80m (42ft)
Height:	6.22m (20.4ft)
Maximum Take-off Weight:	27,415kg (60,439lb)
Powerplant:	2 x Xian WS9 turbofans
Thrust:	9325kg (20,515lb) each
Maximum Speed:	1808km/h (1122mph)
Ceiling:	15,500m (50,850ft)
Range:	900km (560 miles)
Armament:	2 x 23mm cannon, wingtip rails for PL-5 AAMs, 2 x C-801 or C-802 (YJ-1) ASMs
Systems:	unknown
Date Deployed:	1993

J-8IIM FINBACK

The J-8 was the first Chinese Air Force jet fighter of domestic design. The overall configuration is a rather straightforward enlargement of the MiG-21/J-7 layout to accommodate two engines. Although it resembled Mikoyan's experimental Ye-152A, contrary to some early reports it was not based on that aircraft. Production began in December 1979, with about 100–150 units of the first configuration entering service. Design work on the improved J-8-2 began in 1980, with production beginning in late 1980. The Jian-8IIM upgrader, co-developed by China and Russia, is the result of a thorough modernization of the F-8M fighter ("M" standing for export-only weaponry in China's weapon designation system). The first flight of this version was conducted on 31 March 1996. It features upgraded electronics systems, the lack of which has disadvantaged China's fighter planes for a long time. The J-8IIM fighter will probably be equipped with Russia's or China's helmet sight and advanced PL-9 and P-73 missiles. Phazotron, a Russian firm, has agreed to provide 150–200 improved Zhuk radars mainly in support of China's new F-8II fighter. These radars can track while scanning on 24 targets, display up to 8 of them, and simultaneously provide fire-control solutions for 2–4 of them.

SPECIFICATIONS

Primary Role:	interceptor
Crew:	1
Contractor:	Shenyang Aircraft Company
Length:	21.6m (70.9ft)
Wingspan:	9.3m (30ft)
Height:	5.4m (17.75ft)
Maximum Take-off Weight:	17,800kg (39,200lb)
Powerplant:	2 x Wopen 13A-II turbojets
Thrust:	6734kg (14,815lb) each
Maximum Speed:	2340km/h (1450mph)
Ceiling:	20,000m (65,616ft)
Range:	1300km (813 miles)
Armament:	2 x 23mm cannon, 4 x PL-2 or PL-7
Systems:	Izmurd ranging radar
Date Deployed:	1979

ALPHA JET

The Dassault-Breguet-Dornier Alpha Jet is a twin-seat subsonic fighter-bomber that due to its conception and versatile characteristics is particularly suitable for supporting air offensive operations, ground operations, as well as for advanced training on bombers, fighters and operational conversion training, with the capability of using different weapon configurations. Its equipment allows it to obtain great efficiency when planning and executing missions. The Head-Up Display (HUD) saves the pilot from looking down into the cockpit to read the instruments, by superimposing data on a clear plate mounted at eye level. The navigation and fire-control computers are precise and permit great flexibility on attack missions. The use of the "AFA" computer makes the planning of a mission simpler, quicker and more efficient. The Alpha Jet 2 is a development of the training aircraft and is optimized for ground attack. It has an integrated weapon system – laser range finder, inertial navigation unit, HUD – allowing it to fulfil either weapon system training missions or ground-attack missions with a great accuracy. The Alpha Jet ATS (Advanced Training System) allows pilots to familiarize themselves with the navigation and attack systems of the latest and future European fighter aircraft.

SPECIFICATIONS

Primary Role:	light attack, advanced trainer
Crew:	2
Contractor:	Dassault-Breguet-Dornier
Length:	12.3m (40.25ft)
Wingspan:	9.14m (30ft)
Height:	4.19m (13ft)
Maximum Take-off Weight:	8000kg (17,637lb)
Powerplant:	2 x SNECMA 04-C6 turbofans
Thrust:	2705kg (5952lb) each
Maximum Speed:	1160km/h (725mph)
Ceiling:	15,240m (50,000ft)
Range:	2600km (1625 miles)
Armament:	mixture of Bl755, Matra F1 gun pod, Belouga, AGM-65 maverick, AIM-9L
Systems:	Radar Warning Receiver (RWR)
Date Deployed:	1977

AMX

The AMX, a joint programme undertaken by Alenia, Aermacchi and Embraer, is an attack aircraft for battlefield interdiction, close air support and reconnaissance. The wings are mounted high, swept back and tapered with square tips. AAMs are usually mounted on the wings. There are two air intakes forward of the wing roots; there is a single exhaust. The fuselage has a pointed nose and bubble canopy. The body widens at the air intakes and tapers to the rear. The tail flats are mid-mounted on the fuselage, swept back and tapered. It is capable of operating at high subsonic speed and low altitude, by day or night, and if necessary from bases with poorly equipped or damaged runways. Its low infrared signature, reduced radar equivalent cross-section and low vulnerability of structure and systems guarantee a high probability of mission success. The integrated ECM, air-to-air missiles and nose-mounted guns provide self-defence capabilities. The AMX-T is a twin-seater, high performance transonic turbofan jet, specifically developed for advanced and fighter lead-in training. It maintains the operational characteristics of the AMX, which is already in operation with the Brazilian and Italian air forces. The AMX-T was selected by the Venezuelan Air Force to replace the old T-2A Buckeyes in the advanced training role.

SPECIFICATIONS

Primary Role:	light bomber/fighter
Crew:	1
Contractor:	Alenia, Aermacchi, Embraer
Length:	13.58m (44.5ft)
Wingspan:	8.84m (29ft)
Height:	4.54m (14.92ft)
Maximum Take-off Weight:	13,027kg (28,660lb)
Powerplant:	1 x Rolls-Royce Spey MK 807
Thrust:	5010kg (11,023lb)
Maximum Speed:	1053km/h (658mph)
Ceiling:	13,000m (42650ft)
Range:	1840km (1150 miles)
Armament:	1 x 20mm cannon, AIM-9L Sidewinder, ELT-555 jamming pod, Belouga, Kormoran
Systems:	FIAR Pointer range-only radar, RWR, ballistic bombsight
Date Deployed:	1989

C-160 TRANSALL

The Transall C-160 first flew in 1963. Production was completed in 1972, but in 1977 the programme was reinstated to produce a "new generation" C-160 for France. The last of these new generation aircraft entered service in 1987. Two turboprop engines are mounted under and extend beyond the wings' leading edges. The fuselage is long, thick and tapered to the rear with a round, solid nose, stepped cockpit and upswept tail section. The tail flats are mid-mounted on a thinned body, equally tapered with blunt tips. The fin is tall and tapered with a blunt tip and a fairing in the leading edge. A variant is the C-160 Gabriel, which features an ELINT subsystem provided by Thomson-CSF Radars & Contre-Mesures for detection, analysis and location of radar sources with a subsystem for detection, interception, classification, listening-in, analysis and location of radio transmitters. Four communications relay aircraft, designation C-160H Astarte, have been delivered to the French Air Force since 1987. The aircrafts' main mission is communications with the submerged nuclear ballistic missile submarines of the French fleet. The aircraft are equipped with unjammable VLF communications including a Rockwell VLF transmitter and a Thales communications centre. The VLF system includes dual trailing wire antennae.

SPECIFICATIONS

Primary Role:	transport, EW, surveillance
Crew:	5
Contractor:	Aerospatiale
Length:	32.4m (106.25ft)
Wingspan:	40m (131.25ft)
Height:	11.67m (38.28ft)
Maximum Take-off Weight:	51,000kg (112,200lb)
Powerplant:	2 x Rolls-Royce Tyne 22
Thrust:	4549kg (10,007lb) each
Maximum Speed:	515km/h (322mph)
Ceiling:	7925m (26,000ft)
Range:	5095km (3184 miles)
Armament:	usually none
Systems:	inertial navigation system, GPS, ELINT, VLF
Date Deployed:	1963

CN-235

The CN-235 is a high-wing, pressurized, twin turbo-prop aircraft with short take-off and landing (STOL) performance that can carry a maximum payload of 6000kg (13,200lb). The CN-235 has been conceived for tactical military transport and is capable of operating from unpaved runways and has excellent low-level flying characteristics for tactical penetration. It can be used to transport up to 48 paratroopers who can exit via either of the two side doors or the rear ramp. The CN-235 is able to carry out high- and low-altitude in-flight drops to forward troops. On medical evacuation missions, the aircraft can transport up to 21 stretchers, plus four medics. Although the CN-235 was initially the result of cooperation between CASA and ITPN of Indonesia, CASA has developed its own series and versions, with increases in weights and performance. CASA's aircraft is thus the product of continuous development, not just in the military sphere, but also in civil areas. The CN-235 is the ideal platform for the development and integration of a wide variety of versions, such as the Maritime Patrol Version (Persuader), electronic warfare, early warning and photo reconnaissance. The CN-235 is undoubtedly a leader in its class, with more than 220 aircraft sold to 29 operators and 500,000 flight hours to date.

SPECIFICATIONS

Primary Role:	light transport
Crew:	3
Contractor:	CASA and ITPN
Length:	21.40m (70.1ft)
Wingspan:	25.81m (84.66ft)
Height:	8.2m (26.9ft)
Maximum Take-off Weight:	16,500kg (36,376lb)
Powerplant:	2 x General Electric CT7-9C turboprops
Thrust:	2610kg (5742lb) each
Maximum Speed:	445km/h (276mph)
Ceiling:	9900m (32,480ft)
Range:	5000km (3125 miles)
Armament:	none
Systems:	ESM/ECM and ELINT/COMINT
Date Deployed:	1986

EUROFIGHTER TYPHOON

Eurofighter is a single-seat, twin-engine combat aircraft which will be used in the air-to-air, air-to-ground and tactical reconnaissance roles. Its design is optimized for air dominance performance with high instantaneous and sustained turn rates, and specific excess power. Special emphasis has been placed on low wing loading, high thrust-to-weight ratio, excellent all-round vision and carefree handling. Eurofighter's high performance is matched by excellent all-round vision and by sophisticated attack, identification and defence systems which include the ECR 90 long-range radar and Infrared Search and Track (IRST) system, advanced medium- and short-range air-to-air missiles and a comprehensive electronic warfare suite. The aircraft is intentionally aerodynamically unstable to provide extremely high levels of agility, reduced drag and enhanced lift. The unstable design cannot be flown by conventional means and the pilot controls the aircraft via a computerised "fly-by-wire" system. The Eurojet EJ200 turbofan engine combines high thrust with low fuel consumption. To reduce ownership costs over Eurofighter Typhoon's in-service life of 25 years or 6000 flying hours, and to ensure maximum availability, the areas of reliability, maintainability and testability have been given equal priority to performance and flight safety.

SPECIFICATIONS

Primary Role:	*multirole fighter*
Crew:	*1*
Contractor:	*BAe, DASA, Alenia, CASA*
Length:	*14.96m (49ft)*
Wingspan:	*10.95m (35.9ft)*
Height:	*5.28m (17.32ft)*
Maximum Take-off Weight:	*21,000kg (46,200lb)*
Powerplant:	*2 x EJ200 turbofans*
Thrust:	*9091kg (20,000lb) each*
Maximum Speed:	*2125km/hr (1328mph)*
Ceiling:	*classified*
Range:	*1389km (868 miles)*
Armament:	*1 x 27mm gun, mix of BVRAAM, SRAAM ,laser-guided bombs, anti-armour weapons*
Systems:	*ECR 90 radar, IRST*
Date Deployed:	*2002*

JAGUAR

The Jaguar has a long sleek fuselage with a large swept tail fin and rudder. The fuselage features a long, pointed, chiselled nose, and the relatively short-span swept wings are shoulder-mounted on the fuselage. The internal jet engines, mounted to the rear of the cockpit, have rectangular air intakes either side of the fuselage behind the cockpit, with their top surfaces forming an extension of the wing. The engine exhausts show prominently under the forward portion of the tail. The rear jetpipes are located forward and below the tailplane which has marked anhedral; the raised bubble canopy is set above the sharply pointed nose. The twin mainwheels of the undercarriage retract into the fuselage. A variety of weapons, including cluster, freefall, retard and laser-guided bombs, as well as rockets, can be carried. Two 30mm cannon are mounted internally. To mark targets for laser-guided weapons, the aircraft carries the thermal imaging and laser designation (TIALD) pod. For self-defence, Sidewinder infrared missiles are carried and the aircraft is fitted with comprehensive electronic countermeasures. With mission data fed into the computer, all the information for a pinpoint attack is relayed to the HUD. From the display, the pilot knows exactly where the target is located and when to release his weapons for maximum effect.

SPECIFICATIONS

Primary Role:	close air support
Crew:	1
Contractor:	Dassault, BAe
Length:	16.83m (55.25ft)
Wingspan:	8.69m (28.5ft)
Height:	4.80m (15.74ft)
Maximum Take-off Weight:	15,000kg (33,000lb)
Powerplant:	2 x Adour 104 turbofans
Thrust:	3320kg (7305lb) each
Maximum Speed:	1593km/h (996mph)
Ceiling:	12,192m (40,000ft)
Range:	3524km (2202 miles)
Armament:	2 x 30mm guns, mix of Matra Magic R550 AAMs, AS 30 ASMs, rockets, bombs
Systems:	ECM, gyroscopic guidance
Date Deployed:	1972

TORNADO F3

The Tornado is a twin-seat, twin-engined, variable geometry aircraft that is supersonic at all altitudes. The wings of the aircraft are high-mounted, variable, swept-back and tapered with angular, blunt tips. There are two turbofan engines inside the body. The air intakes are diagonal and box-like alongside the fuselage forward of the wing roots. There are twin exhausts. The fuselage is solid and has a needle nose. The body thickens midsection and tapers to the tail section. The tail is tall, swept-back and has a tapered fin with a curved tip and a step in the leading edge. The flats are large, mid-mounted on the body, swept-back and tapered with blunt tips. The Tornado F3 air defence fighter has an 80 percent commonality with the Tornado GR1 strike/attack aircraft. The Tornado F3 is optimized for long-range interception, for which it carries four Skyflash radar-guided missiles and four AIM 9 Sidewinder infrared AAMs, plus internally mounted 27mm Mauser cannons. Tornado F3s are being equipped with the new Joint Tactical Information Distribution System. Operating in conjunction with E-3D Sentry airborne early warning aircraft and other allied fighters, the crew can thus select its own target and move to within "kill" distance without using the fighter's own search radar until the very last moment.

SPECIFICATIONS

Primary Role:	*air defence fighter*
Crew:	*2*
Contractor:	*Panavia Aircraft GmbH*
Length:	*16.72m (54.85ft)*
Wingspan:	*13.91m (45.63ft) fully forward*
Height:	*5.95m (19.52ft)*
Maximum Take-off Weight:	*28,000kg (61,600lb)*
Powerplant:	*2 x RB199-34R turbofans*
Thrust:	*6582kg (14,480lb) each*
Maximum Speed:	*2336km/h (1452mph)*
Ceiling:	*15,240m (50,000ft)*
Range:	*3900km (2437 miles)*
Armament:	*2 x 27mm cannon, Sidewinder, HARM, AGM-65, ALARM, Paveway, Apache,*
Systems:	*Joint Tactical Information Distribution System*
Date Deployed:	*1984*

TORNADO GR1

The GR1 originated from a UK Staff Requirement in 1969 which called for a medium-range, low-level, counter-air strike aircraft, with the further capabilities of interdiction and reconnaissance. The Tornado first saw action during the Gulf War of 1991, when several were lost as a result of daring ultra-low-level missions to close Iraqi airfields. The proliferation of anti-aircraft defences in Iraq, Bosnia and elsewhere that the UK might be called on to operate in has meant that the standard GR1 is in danger of not being able to fulfil the covert deep-penetration operations that it was designed for. Furthermore, the advance of air-delivered weapons has meant that strike aircraft need to become ever more sophisticated, especially given the fears of "collateral damage" or accidentally hitting civilian targets. The Tornado GR1 strike/attack aircraft is capable of carrying a wide range of conventional stores, including the JP233 anti-airfield weapon, the ALARM anti-radar missile and laser-guided bombs. The reconnaissance version, designated the GR1A, retains the full operational capability of the GR1. The GR1B, equipped with Sea Eagle air-to-surface missiles, undertakes the anti-surface shipping role. For self-defence, the Tornado carries Sidewinder air-to-air missiles and is fitted with twin internal 27mm cannons.

SPECIFICATIONS

Primary Role:	strike/attack aircraft
Crew:	2
Contractor:	Panavia Aircraft GmbH
Length:	16.72m (54.85ft)
Wingspan:	13.91m (45.63ft) fully forward
Height:	5.95m (19.52ft)
Maximum Take-off Weight:	28,000kg (61,600lb)
Powerplant:	2 x RB199-34R turbofans
Thrust:	6582kg (14,480lb) each
Maximum Speed:	2336km/h (1452mph)
Ceiling:	15,240m (50,000ft)
Range:	3900km (2418 miles)
Armament:	2 x 27mm cannon, Sidewinder, HARM, AGM-65, ALARM, Sea Eagle, Paveway, Apache, JP233
Systems:	Sideways Looking Infrared, Linescan surveillance system
Date Deployed:	1980

TORNADO GR4

A mid-life update (MLU) programme was completed by the end of 1998 which gave the aircraft the capability to carry advanced weapons such as the anti-armour weapon "Brimstone" and the stand-off attack missile "Storm Shadow". The updated aircraft is designated Tornado GR4. The last of the updates is scheduled for early 2003. The MLU will allow the RAF's Tornados to serve well into the twenty-first century. The airframe's life is to be extended as a result of more advanced technology and this will avoid the necessity of expensive refits or the acquisition of new aircraft. In addition to the existing range of weaponry, such as laser-guided bombs and anti-radar missiles, the GR4 will be able to operate new equipment and will also be capable of using the Sea Eagle anti-shipping missile; whereas only the relatively small number of Tornado GR1Bs are currently fitted for maritime strike. The actual payload, speed, altitude and other performance characteristics of the GR4 will remain much the same as for the GR1. What will change is the overall capability of the aircraft. The ability to see in the dark when using FLIR and NVGs will permit GR4s to fly at terrain-following height without navigation lights or radar emissions. This makes the GR4 more stealthy, enhancing its chances of covert deep penetration and mission survival.

SPECIFICATIONS

Primary Role:	all-weather strike aircraft
Crew:	2
Contractor:	Panavia Aircraft GmbH
Length:	16.72m (54.85ft)
Wingspan:	13.91m (45.63ft) fully forward
Height:	5.95m (19.52ft)
Maximum Take-off Weight:	28,000kg (61,600lb)
Powerplant:	2 x RB199-34R turbofans
Thrust:	6582kg (14,480lb) each
Maximum Speed:	2336km/h (1452mph)
Ceiling:	15,240m (50,000ft)
Range:	3900km (2418 miles)
Armament:	2 x 27mm cannon, Sidewinder, HARM, AGM-65, ALARM, Sea Eagle, Paveway, Apache, JP233
Systems:	Forward-Looking Infrared (FLIR), Defensive Aids
Date Deployed:	1998

MIRAGE IV

In the mid-1950s, the French decided to develop their own nuclear deterrent force. As with other nuclear powers, France would eventually develop land-based and submarine-based missiles, and a strategic bomber, the Mirage IV. Work that would lead to the Mirage IV began in 1957. Dassault met the French government requirement for a strategic bomber by scaling up the Mirage III 50 percent in linear dimensions, doubling weight and wing area. The prototype Mirage IV first flew in June 1959, and had Atar 09C engines and a taller fin than later production aircraft. The second prototype flew in October 1961. The weapon for which the Mirage IV was designed, the 60-kiloton AN-22 nuclear weapon, fits into a recess in the fuselage. This weapon was modified after late 1967 to be parachute-retarded, when it was realized that the Mirage IV would not be able to penetrate Soviet airspace at high altitude. The Mirage IV obtained a new lease on life in the bomber role when 18 were rebuilt as Mirage IVPs ("P" for "Penetration") to carry the ASMP stand-off missile instead of the AN-22. This meant a considerable upgrade of the aircraft's avionics and the addition of a centre pylon to handle the ASMP. By 2000, all Mirage IV bombers had been retired, but five Mirage IVR variants remained in service.

SPECIFICATIONS

Primary Role:	bomber/reconnaissance aircraft
Crew:	2
Contractor:	Dassault
Length:	23.50m (77.1ft)
Wingspan:	11.85m (38.9ft)
Height:	5.65m (18.5ft)
Maximum Take-off Weight:	31,600kg (70,000lb)
Powerplant:	2 x Atar 9K-50 turbojets
Thrust:	14,430kg (31,746lb) each
Maximum Speed:	2335km/h (1451mph)
Ceiling:	20,000m (65,600ft)
Range:	3200km (2000 miles)
Armament:	60kt nuclear bomb, ASMP nuclear weapon, Martel ASMs, bombs, rockets
Systems:	Cytano II radar, RWR, Agave radar
Date Deployed:	1962

MIRAGE 2000B & C

The wings of the Mirage 2000 are low-mounted, delta shaped with clipped tips. There is one turbofan engine mounted in the fuselage, semicircular air intakes alongside the fuselage forward of the wings, a large, single exhaust which protrudes past the tail, and the fuselage is tube-shaped with a pointed nose and bubble canopy. The fin is swept-back and tapered with a clipped tip. The aircraft are fitted with the RDI pulse doppler radar and Super 530D semi-active AAMs with look-down and shoot-down capability. They also feature Magic 2 heat-seeking air-to-air combat missiles and an integrated electronic warfare suite. They are multirole and can also carry out air-to-ground missions with conventional bombs and rockets, although this is only a secondary assignment for them under the current French Air Force structure. Mirage 2000C/Bs can be refuelled in flight and were deployed with coalition forces in the Gulf War, and in the Bosnia and Kosovo conflicts in the 1990s. The Mirage 2000-5F version is a Mirage 2000C upgraded to Mirage 2000-5 standard with the RDY multitarget/multishoot capability, active seeker Mica missiles, and new cockpit displays and processors. At the beginning of 2000, the last of 37 Mirage 2000-5Fs ordered on the current upgrade contract were delivered.

SPECIFICATIONS

Primary Role:	*multirole fighter*
Crew:	*1*
Contractor:	*Dassault*
Length:	*14.36m (47.1ft)*
Wingspan:	*9.13m (29.9ft)*
Height:	*5.2m (17ft)*
Maximum Take-off Weight:	*17,000kg (37,400lb)*
Powerplant:	*1 x SNECMA M53-P2 turbofan*
Thrust:	*9720kg (21,385lb)*
Maximum Speed:	*1220km/h (762mph)*
Ceiling:	*16,500m (54,133ft)*
Range:	*3704km (2315 miles)*
Armament:	*2 x 30mm cannon, Super 530D, Magic 2 AAMs*
Systems:	*RDI pulse doppler radar, RDY multitarget/multishoot capability*
Date Deployed:	*1984*

MIRAGE 2000N

The Mirage 2000 strike aircraft is very similar to the Mirage III/5 and 50 variants, though it is not a variant of these aircraft but an entirely new model with advanced interceptor controls. In its secondary ground-attack role, the Mirage 2000 carries laser-guided missiles, rockets and bombs. The prime assignment of the two-seat Mirage 2000N is the nuclear strike mission, and as such has a dedicated WSO (weapon system operator) rear crew station to allow it to fulfil its strategic role. It features a special redundant navigation system with the Antilope terrain-following radar, allowing it to fly "blind" as low as 61m (200ft) above ground level under fully automatic guidance from the system. The cockpit is compatible with night vision goggles. The Mirage 2000N can be refuelled in flight and can also deliver unguided bombs and rockets as a secondary mission (the Mirage 2000D is a conventional strike derivative of the Mirage 2000N). Due to its strategic capabilities, the Mirage 2000N is not licensed for export. Laser-guided weapons can be delivered with the PDL-CT laser designator pod, which is fitted with an infrared camera. The Mirage 2000D is also able to carry out all-weather blind attacks on coordinates. Some 86 Mirage 2000Ds have been ordered by the French Air Force.

SPECIFICATIONS

Primary Role:	*nuclear strike aircraft*
Crew:	*2*
Contractor:	*Dassault*
Length:	*14.36m (47.11ft)*
Wingspan:	*9.13m (29.94ft)*
Height:	*5.30m (17.38ft)*
Maximum Take-off Weight:	*16,500kg (36,300lb)*
Powerplant:	*1 x SNECMA M 53 P2 turbofan*
Thrust:	*9700kg (21,340lb)*
Maximum Speed:	*2236km/h (1397mph)*
Ceiling:	*16,500m (54,133ft)*
Range:	*3335km (2084 miles)*
Armament:	*ASMP nuclear weapon*
Systems:	*fly-by-wire, inertial navigation systems, Antilope radar, GPS, integrated countermeasures, laser designator*
Date Deployed:	*1982*

MIRAGE F-1

ollowing on the Mirage F-2, which was a revival of the classic arrow-wing design with stabilizers, the Mirage F-1 is a defence and air superiority single-seater aircraft. This revival was made possible by technological advances which permit manufacture of ultra-thin but robust wings, enabling flight performance at supersonic speeds equivalent to that of delta wings (the wings are high-mounted, swept-back and tapered). The integrity of the fuselage structure allows the aircraft to carry a maximum amount of fuel. The Mirage F-1 prototype made its maiden flight on 23 December 1966, at Melun-Villaroche (the Seine-et-Marne region of France). Commissioned by the French Air Force in 1973, more than 700 Mirage F-1s have been sold to 11 countries. The Dassault Mirage F-1C was the standard French fighter before the Mirage 2000 entered service in the air force in 1984. Missiles are usually mounted at the wing tips. There is one turbojet engine in the body, semicircular air intakes alongside the body forward of the wing roots, and there is a single exhaust. The fuselage is long, slender, pointed nose with a blunt tail. There are two small belly fins under the tail section and a bubble canopy. The flats are mid-mounted on the fuselage, swept-back, and tapered with blunt tips. There is also a reconnaissance version, the F-1CR.

SPECIFICATIONS

Primary Role:	*close air support/attack*
Crew:	*1*
Contractor:	*Dassault*
Length:	*14.94m (49ft)*
Wingspan:	*8.4m (27.6ft)*
Height:	*4.50m (14.76ft)*
Maximum Take-off Weight:	*16,200kg (35,640lb)*
Powerplant:	*1 x SNECMA Atar 9K50*
Thrust:	*6800kg (14,960kg)*
Maximum Speed:	*2238km/h (1390mph)*
Ceiling:	*15,850m (52,000ft)*
Range:	*1400km (875 miles)*
Armament:	*2 x 30mm cannon, Super 530, Magic 550, Sidewinder AAMs, AM 39 Exocet, AS.30L ASMs*
Systems:	*Cyrano IVM radar, RWR, Desire digital video recce pod, ECM*
Date Deployed:	*1973*

RAFALE

The Rafale programme is composed of three versions of this multi-purpose aircraft: the single-seater (Rafale C), two-seater (Rafale B) and single-seater navy version (Rafale M). These three versions are fitted with the same engines, navigation and attack system, aircraft management system and flight control system. They are all able to perform all types of missions from ground-attack to air superiority. The first production aircraft flew for the first time on 4 December 1998, and total orders stand at 294 aircraft. Its excellent flying characteristics stem from the "delta-canard" aerodynamic concept combining a delta wing and an active foreplane judiciously located in relation to the wing so as to optimize aerodynamic efficiency and stability control without impeding the pilot's visibility. The Rafale C is a multirole fighter with a fully integrated weapons and navigation systems, making use of the latest technology and is capable of outstanding performance on multiple target air-to-air missions and air-to-surface missions deep behind enemy lines. The Rafale B retains most of the elements of the single-seater version, and its weapon and navigation system is exactly the same. The Rafale M also carries the same weapons. Designed for aircraft carriers, it retains most of the flying qualities of the other versions.

SPECIFICATIONS

Primary Role:	multirole fighter
Crew:	1
Contractor:	Dassault
Length:	15.30m (50.2ft)
Wingspan:	10.9m (35.75ft)
Height:	5.34m (17.5ft)
Maximum Take-off Weight:	21,500kg (47,399lb)
Powerplant:	2 x SNECMA M88-2 turbofans
Thrust:	9954kg (21,900lb) each
Maximum Speed:	classified
Ceiling:	classified
Range:	3706km (2316 miles)
Armament:	1 X 30mm cannon, ASMP nuclear weapon, Mica AAMs, Exocet ASMs
Systems:	SPECTRA defensive system, RBE2 electronic scanning radar
Date Deployed:	2001

SUPER ETENDARD

The Super Etendard is a carrier-based single-seat strike fighter first introduced into service in 1978. It is an updated version of the Etendard IVM. Based on experience gained during the Korean war (1950–53), the French authorities drew up specifications for a light interceptor aircraft. This definition was rapidly assimilated into a programme for a light tactical bomber that could also fulfil an air superiority mission. The naval single-seater combat aircraft, Dassault Super Etendard, is different to the Etendard IVM. Main modifications include updating of the weapons system through the installation (a first for a French production aircraft) of a modern navigation and combat management system. The aircraft prototype made its maiden flight on 28 October 1974 at Istres (the Bouches-du-Rhône region of France). The French Navy commissioned the plane for the first time in 1977, and 71 aircraft are now in service on the aircraft carriers *Foch* and *Clemenceau*. It was the Super Etendard, armed with Exocet anti-ship missiles and flown by Argentinian pilots (14 aircraft in all), that proved its combat effectiveness during the Falklands War with Britain in 1982. The Super Etendard will be replaced by the naval version of the Rafale multirole combat aircraft during the early years of the twenty-first century.

SPECIFICATIONS

Primary Role:	carrier-borne strike fighter
Crew:	1
Contractor:	Dassault
Length:	14.31m (46.9ft)
Wingspan:	9.6m (31.5ft)
Height:	3.86m (12.75ft)
Maximum Take-off Weight:	12,000kg (26,455lb)
Powerplant:	1 x SNECMA Atar turbojet
Thrust:	5011kg (11,025lb)
Maximum Speed:	1173km/h (733mph)
Ceiling:	13,700M (45,000ft)
Range:	1700km (1062 miles)
Armament:	2 x 30mm cannon, Magic 550 AAM, Exocet ASM
Systems:	Barracuda and Phimat jamming pods, Anémone radar. Drax radar detector
Date Deployed:	1978

CANBERRA PR9

The first jet bomber to serve with the Royal Air Force (RAF), the English Electric Canberra was designed with no defensive armament, relying instead on high speed, an operational ceiling of 14,630m (48,000ft) and great manoeuvrability to avoid opposing fighter aircraft. The fact that the Canberra is still in service today is testimony to the quality of the original design. Currently the RAF operates two versions of the aircraft, the T4 is a dual control trainer, and dedicated reconnaissance missions are undertaken by the venerable Canberra PR9, specialist aircraft that contribute significantly to meeting the RAF's reconnaissance task through the use of a wide range of onboard vertical and oblique cameras. The first RAF reconnaissance version, the PR3, first flew on 19 March 1950. The main difference between it and other Canberra versions was a 356mm (14in) extension to the forward fuselage to accommodate an additional fuel tank, a camera bay and a flare bay. Deliveries to the first squadron, No 540 at RAF Benson, began in December 1952. The PR7 was an improved version of the aircraft, but the definitive version was the PR9, which became operational with the RAF's No 58 Squadron. In 1962, PR9s were used to photograph Soviet shipping movements during the Cuban missile crisis.

SPECIFICATIONS

Primary Role:	reconnaissance
Crew:	2
Contractor:	BAe
Length:	20.32m (66.6ft)
Wingspan:	20.67m (67.8ft)
Height:	4.77m (15.6ft)
Maximum Take-off Weight:	24,977kg (54,950lb)
Powerplant:	2 x Avon 109 turbojets
Thrust:	6741kg (14,800lb) each
Maximum Speed:	827km/h (517mph)
Ceiling:	14,630m (48,000ft)
Range:	5840km (3650 miles)
Armament:	none
Systems:	F49/F96 Mk4 Survey camera, LORAN air direction finder, ALQ-167 jamming suite, AIRPASS III Blue Parrot radar
Date Deployed:	1960

HARRIER GR7

This is the latest in the long line of Harrier "Jump Jets" originating from the 1960s. The second-generation GR5 and GR7 versions replaced the original Harrier GR3s in the late 1980s and early 1990s. The GR7 is essentially a licence-built, American-designed AV-8B Harrier II fitted with RAF-specific systems as well as other changes, including additional underwing pylons for Sidewinder missiles. The improved design of the GR7 allows the aircraft to carry twice the load of a GR3 over the same distance or the same load twice the distance. The first flight of the Harrier GR7 was in 1989, and deliveries to RAF squadrons began in 1990. A total of 96 aircraft were ordered. Fully operational with three frontline squadrons and the Operational Conversion Unit, the aircraft carries Forward-Looking Infrared (FLIR) equipment which, when used in conjunction with the pilot's night vision goggles (NVGs), provides a night, low-altitude capability. The Harrier is also ideally suited to medium-level operations where it utilizes its highly accurate angle rate bombing system (ARBS), which employs a TV and laser dual mode tracker. The Harrier remains a highly versatile aircraft and can easily be deployed to remote forward operating locations. The Harrier T10, a two-seat trainer version of the GR7, came into service in 1995.

SPECIFICATIONS

Primary Role:	*ground-attack fighter*
Crew:	*1*
Contractor:	*BAe*
Length:	*14.36m (47.1ft)*
Wingspan:	*9.25m (30.3ft)*
Height:	*3.55m (11.6ft)*
Maximum Take-off Weight:	*14,061kg (31,000lb)*
Powerplant:	*1 x Pegasus Mk 105 turbofan*
Thrust:	*9773kg (21,500lb)*
Maximum Speed:	*1065km/h (661mph)*
Ceiling:	*15,000m (49,000ft)*
Range:	*2202km (1376 miles)*
Armament:	*2 x 25mm cannon, 16 Mk 82 or 6 Mk 83 bombs, BL-755 cluster bombs, Maverick ASM*
Systems:	*FLIR, ARBS, dual mode tracker (DMT)*
Date Deployed:	*1990*

HAWK

The Hawk is a light-attack and trainer aircraft which, through a continuing update and modernization programme, is still known as one of the world's best aircraft in its class. With a crew of two, it features low-mounted, swept-back wings that are tapered with curved tips. One turbofan engine is located inside the body, with semi-circular air intakes alongside the body forward of the wing roots and a single exhaust. The top line of the fuselage curves up from the pointed nose to incorporate the long, clear cockpit canopy, then slopes down to the jetpipe, giving a humped appearance, with slightly swept vertical and horizontal tail surfaces. The Royal Air Force (RAF) bought 175 Hawk Mk T1 aircraft in the late 1970s. RAF Hawks are used in advanced jet and weapons training. Other user countries include Brunei, Finland, Indonesia, Kenya, Kuwait, Malaysia, Oman, Saudi Arabia, South Korea and the United Arab Emirates. In the current RAF training programme, the Hawk T1 is used to teach operational tactics, air-to-air and air-to-ground firing, air combat and low-level operating procedures. To supplement the Tornado F3 force, some Hawk T1A advanced trainers have an additional task as point defence fighters. In this role they carry Sidewinder air-to-air missiles (AAMs) and a 30mm Aden cannon.

SPECIFICATIONS

Primary Role:	*trainer/ground-attack aircraft*
Crew:	*2*
Contractor:	*BAe*
Length:	*11.2m (36.6ft)*
Wingspan:	*9.39m (30.75ft)*
Height:	*3.9m (13ft)*
Maximum Take-off Weight:	*5700kg (12,566lb)*
Powerplant:	*1 x Rolls-Royce Turbomeca Adour turbofan*
Thrust:	*2591kg (5700lb)*
Maximum Speed:	*1010km/h (627mph)*
Ceiling:	*13,700m (44,947ft)*
Range:	*2917km (1823 miles)*
Armament:	*removable 30mm gun pod, five hardpoints; 3000kg (6614lb) warload, AIM-9 Sidewinder*
Systems:	*APG-66H, LINS 300*
Date Deployed:	*1976*

NIMROD MRA4

The Nimrod resembles the DH Comet, from which it derived: long "double bubble" fuselage with the cockpit built into the steeply raked nose. The fuselage tailcone extends well beyond the fin and rudder to house a magnetic anomaly detector (MAD) unit. An inflight refuelling probe projects from the fuselage above the cockpit. In July 1996 British Aerospace was selected as the prime contractor to supply a complete package of 21 mission-equipped Nimrod 2000 aircraft. A contract was awarded in December 1996, under which existing MR Mk 2 aircraft fuselage and empennage structures would be overhauled and reassembled, with redesigned wings and current-technology BR710 turbofan engines. The majority of the air vehicle systems have been replaced, including the flight deck, which will accommodate a reduced cockpit crew complement of two, facilitated by automated flight systems using modified Airbus A340 technology. The mission system, which is at the heart of the weapon system, is entirely new. The cabin interior is totally refitted to suit the new mission systems layout. This is therefore a new aircraft, not a refurbished one. In early 1998 the aircraft was renamed from Nimrod 2000 to Nimrod Maritime Reconnaissance and Attack Mk4 – Nimrod MRA4.

SPECIFICATIONS

Primary Role:	maritime reconnaissance
Crew:	13
Contractor:	BAe
Length:	38.63m (126.75ft)
Wingspan:	35m (114.9ft)
Height:	9m (29.6ft)
Maximum Take-off Weight:	80,510kg (177,500lb)
Powerplant:	4 x RB168-20 250 turbofans
Thrust:	5518kg (12,140lb) each
Maximum Speed:	926km/h (575mph)
Ceiling:	12,800m (41,994ft)
Range:	8340km (5212 miles)
Armament:	torpedoes, bombs and depth charges, Sidewinder AAMs
Systems:	tactical command system, armament control system, 2000MR radar, ESM, FLIR, MAD
Date Deployed:	2005

NIMROD MR2

The Nimrod MR2 is a maritime patrol aircraft used for maritime surface surveillance and anti-submarine warfare. Carrying a crew of 13, the aircraft is fitted with radar and magnetic and acoustic detection equipment. The Nimrod maritime patrol aircraft can also assist in search and rescue operations by searching for survivors, giving guidance to rescue craft at the scene, and dropping survival equipment if needed. Equipment includes an advanced search radar, offering greater range and sensitivity coupled with a higher data processing rate; a new acoustic processing system which is compatible with a wide range of existing and projected sonobuoys; and early warning support measures (EWSM) equipment in a pod at each wingtip. Aircraft deployed to Ascension Island during the 1982 Falklands campaign were fitted with Sidewinder air-to-air missiles (AAMs) for self-defence. Air-to-air refuelling probes were fitted at that time to 16 aircraft (redesignated MR Mk 2P), making possible flights of up to 19 hours. Ample space and power is available in the basic Nimrod design to accept additional or alternative sensors such as sideways-looking infrared linescan, low-light level TV and digital processing of intercepted signals. The MR2 fleet will be replaced by Nimrod MRA4 in a refurbishment programme.

SPECIFICATIONS

Primary Role:	*anti-submarine patrol aircraft*
Crew:	*13*
Contractor:	*BAe*
Length:	*38.63m (126.75ft)*
Wingspan:	*35m (114.9ft)*
Height:	*9m (29.6ft)*
Maximum Take-off Weight:	*80,510kg (177,500lb)*
Powerplant:	*4 x RB168-20 250 turbojets*
Thrust:	*5518kg (12,140lb) each*
Maximum Speed:	*926km/h (575mph)*
Ceiling:	*12,800m (41,994ft)*
Range:	*8340km (5212 miles)*
Armament:	*Sidewinder AAMs, Harpoon ASMs, torpedoes*
Systems:	*EWSM, Replacement Acoustic Processor, Searchwater radar*
Date Deployed:	*1979*

NIMROD R1

O riginally designed as a maritime patrol and anti-sub-marine aircraft, the Nimrod is less well known for its secondary role. The original maritime equipment was removed from the airframe, and replaced with a highly sophisticated and sensitive suite of systems used for reconnaissance and the gathering of electronic intelligence. The ability of the Nimrod to loiter for long periods, following a high-speed dash to the required area of operation, make the aircraft ideally suited to this task. The Nimrod Rls are externally distinguishable from the maritime reconnaissance version by the absence of the magnetic anomaly detection tail booms and a distinctive pod on the leading edge of the port wing. Inflight refuelling probes were added in 1982. There is a powerful searchlight on the starboard wing, mounted on a fuel tank called the 4A tank. The searchlight is seven-million candle power and cannot be struck on the ground for more than a few seconds or the heat generated destroys the searchlight. The Nimrod R1 has four Rolls-Royce Spey 250 series twin spool bypass jet engines giving 5518kg (12,140lb) of thrust each. Maximum speed is 926km/h (575mph) and cruise speed is just below 800km/h (500mph). Mission endurance is around eight hours without aerial tanking.

SPECIFICATIONS

Primary Role:	*electronic inteliigence gathering*
Crew:	*12*
Contractor:	*BAe*
Length:	*38.63m (126.75ft)*
Wingspan:	*35m (114.9ft)*
Height:	*9m (29.6ft)*
Maximum Take-off Weight:	*80,000kg (176,000lb)*
Powerplant:	*4 x Rolls-Royce RB168-20 Spey 250 turbofans*
Thrust:	*5518kg (12,140lb) each*
Maximum Speed:	*926km/h (575mph)*
Ceiling:	*12,800m (41,994ft)*
Range:	*8340km (5212 miles)*
Armament:	*none*
Systems:	*Ferranti 1600D computer, Loral electronic support measures (ESM) pods*
Date Deployed:	*1969*

SEA HARRIER

The Sea Harrier is optimized for air-to-air combat with secondary missions of surveillance, air-to-sea and air-to-ground attack. The FA2 is the latest version in service with the Royal Navy (45 aircraft). The aircraft is able to detect and destroy threats before the launch of an attack using long-range weapon systems with look-down and shoot-down tactical capability. A Smiths Industries weapon stores management system ensures the correct selection and release of weapons. The aircraft has five weapons stations. Weapons are mounted on launchers: Raytheon LAU-106A ejection-launchers and Varo LAU-7 rail launchers. The FA2 is equipped with the Raytheon AIM-120A advanced medium-range air-to-air missile (AMRAAM), which is an all-weather, fire-and-forget missile equipped with an active radar seeker and range of over 80km (50 miles). The AIM-9 Sidewinder air-to-air missile (AAM) provides the Harrier with capability for firing at close range at an approaching enemy aircraft in a dogfight. The Sea Harrier's anti-ship missile is the Sea Eagle, a fire-and-forget sea-skimming missile with active radar homing and a range of over 80km (50 miles). It can carry the ALARM anti-radiation missile, which can be deployed in direct attack mode against a radar target or in loiter mode, where the missile waits for the hostile radar to emit.

SPECIFICATIONS

Primary Role:	carrier-borne multirole fighter
Crew:	1
Contractor:	BAe
Length:	14.17m (46.5ft)
Wingspan:	7.70m (25.25ft)
Height:	3.71m (12.1ft)
Maximum Take-off Weight:	11,880kg (26,136lb)
Powerplant:	1 x Rolls-Royce Pegasus turbofan
Thrust:	9773kg (21,500lb)
Maximum Speed:	1200mph (750 miles)
Ceiling:	15,240m (50,000ft)
Range:	1500km (937 miles)
Armament:	2 x 30mm cannon, AMRAAM, AIM-7M AAMs, Sea Eagle ASM, ALARM
Systems:	pulse Doppler radar, TACAN, IPG-100F GPS
Date Deployed:	1993

TRISTAR

The RAF operates a number of Tristar aircraft in the transport role. The Tristar C2s are dedicated transport aircraft and can carry 265 passengers and 16 tonnes (35,000lb) of freight over ranges in excess of 6400km (4000 miles). The other two variants, the K1 and the KC1, are dual role and capable of providing air-to-air refuelling from a pair of centerline fuselage hoses. The K1 can carry 204 passengers; however, the KC1 has a large freight door and can carry 20 cargo pallets, 196 passengers or a combination of mixed freight and passengers. The VC10 and Tristar fleets are based at RAF Brize Norton in Oxfordshire, England. Powerplants consist of two engines in underwing nacelles and one engine mounted on top of the fuselage forward of the swept fin, with the jet efflux below the rudder through the tail cone. The Tristar has a circular, wide-body fuselage with low-set wings at the midway point, and swept tailplane low set either side of the rear fuselage below the fin. Refuelling pods are located under the wings. The KC1 aerial tanker variant has a large portside cargo door and tanks installed under the cabin floor to carry a total capacity of 13,636kg (30,000lb) of fuel. It has twin hose and drogue units in the rear fuselage and an inflight refuelling probe. When not a tanker it can also carry passengers.

SPECIFICATIONS

Primary Role:	transport/tanker
Crew:	4
Contractor:	Lockheed Martin
Length:	50.09m (164.3ft)
Wingspan:	50.17m (164.6ft)
Height:	16.87m (55.3ft)
Maximum Take-off Weight:	224,980kg (496,000lb)
Powerplant:	3 x Rolls-Royce RB211-524B4 turbofans
Thrust:	22,727kg (50,000lb) each
Maximum Speed:	964km/h (602mph)
Ceiling:	13,105m (42,995ft)
Range:	7783km (4864 miles)
Armament:	none
Systems:	Collins flight control system, Sperry air data computer
Date Deployed:	1985

KFIR

The Kfir (which means lion cub) is basically a redesigned Mirage 5 with a canard mounted on the air intake. The wings are low-mounted, delta-shaped with a sawtooth in the leading edges. There are small canards mounted on the air intakes with one turbojet engine inside the fuselage. There are semi-circular air intakes alongside the fuselage, with a large, single exhaust. The fuselage is tube-shaped with a long, solid, pointed nose. The body widens at the air intakes. There is a bubble canopy flush with the spine. The tail has no tail flats. The fin is swept-back and tapered with a prominent step in the leading edge. The Kfir-C7, the definitive single-seat version introduced in 1983, is based on the Kfir-C2 with a specially adapted version of the J79-GEJ1E engine with some 454kg (1000lb) more afterburning thrust. This type has two extra hardpoints and a number of advanced features including capability for the carriage and use of "smart" weapons, Elta EL/M-2021B pulse doppler radar, a revised cockpit with more sophisticated electronics and hands on throttle and stick (HOTAS) controls, and pro-vision for inflight refueling. Maximum take-off weight is increased by 1540kg (3395lb), but combat radius and (more importantly) thrust-to-weight ratio are improved to a marked degree.

SPECIFICATIONS

Primary Role:	multirole fighter
Crew:	1
Contractor:	Israel Aircraft Industries
Length:	15.65m (51.3ft)
Wingspan:	8.22m (26.96ft)
Height:	4.55m (14.9ft)
Maximum Take-off Weight:	16,500kg (36,300lb)
Powerplant:	1 x J79-J1E turbojet
Thrust:	5405kg (11,890lb)
Maximum Speed:	2426km/h (1516mph)
Ceiling:	unknown
Range:	776km (485 miles)
Armament:	2 x 30mm cannon, Magic 550 AIM-9, Shafrir or Python AAMs
Systems:	Elta EL/M-2021B pulse doppler radar, HOTAS (hands on throttle and stick) controls
Date Deployed:	1973

F-2

The F-2 is the replacement for Japan's ageing, domestic F-1 fighter. The cooperatively developed and produced Japanese F-2 single-engine fighter (FS-X) has performance capabilities roughly comparable to those of the US F-16, but costs over three times as much and about the same as the larger two-engine F-15. The F-2 Support Fighter is a multirole, single-engine fighter aircraft produced for the Japan Air Self Defense Force. It was co-developed and is now being co-produced by Mitsubishi Heavy Industries (MHI) of Japan and Lockheed Martin Aeronautics Company (principal US subcontractor to MHI). Based on the design of the Lockheed Martin Aeronautics Company F-16C/D Fighting Falcon, the F-2 is customized to the unique requirements of the Japan Defense Agency. Although capable of both air-to-air and air-to-surface roles, the F-2 emphasizes the air-to-surface role because its primary mission is sea lane protection. The F-2 has a wing area enlarged approximately 25 percent compared to the F-16's wing, allowing more internal fuel storage and two more weapon store stations. The wing is made from graphite epoxy using state-of-the-art composite technology to maximize strength while minimizing weight. In addition to the larger wing area, the F-2 fuselage has also been enlarged by 406mm (16in).

SPECIFICATIONS

Primary Role:	*multirole fighter*
Crew:	*1*
Contractor:	*Mitsubishi, Lockheed Martin*
Length:	*15.52m (50.9ft)*
Wingspan:	*10.8m (35.4ft)*
Height:	*4.96m (16.2ft)*
Maximum Take-off Weight:	*22,272kg (49,000lb)*
Powerplant:	*1 x GE F110-129 turbofan*
Thrust:	*unknown*
Maximum Speed:	*2125km/h (1320mph)*
Ceiling:	*unknown*
Range:	*833km (521 miles)*
Armament:	*1 x 20mm gun, Sparrow & Sidewinder AAMs, ASM-1 & ASM-2 anti-ship missiles*
Systems:	*active phased-array, multi-function display (MFD), HUD*
Date Deployed:	*2000*

A-50 MAINSTAY

The A-50 Mainstay is based on a stretched Ilyushin Il-76 transport combined with an upgraded "Flat Jack" radar system. Developed to replace the Tu-126 Moss (a variant of the Bear bomber), the Mainstay first flew in 1980 with about 40 produced by 1992. The Mainstay is not as sophisticated as its Western counterpart, the E-3 Sentry, but provides Russian fighter regiments with an airborne control capability over both land and water. Mainstays have been used by the Russian Air Force at bases in the Kola Peninsula and for observing Allied air operations during the 1991 Gulf War. In 1994 NATO proposed making the E-3 Sentry and the Mainstay interoperable to enable Russia to provide AEW&C support to future United Nations or coalition operations. The aircraft's wings are high-mounted, swept-back, and tapered with blunt tips. There are four turbofan engines mounted on pylons under and extending beyond the wings' leading edges. The fuselage is long, round and tapered to the rear with a radome on the chin. There is a saucer type radome on top of the aircraft. The aircraft can stay aloft without refueling for four to six hours and can remain airborne for another four hours with mid-air refueling. The radar has a detection range of up to 800km (500 miles) and can track 200 targets simultaneously.

SPECIFICATIONS

Primary Role:	airborne early warning
Crew:	15
Contractor:	Ilyushin/Beriev
Length:	46.59m (152.9ft)
Wingspan:	50.5m (165.6ft)
Height:	14.76m (48.5ft)
Maximum Take-off Weight:	190,000kg (418,000lb)
Powerplant:	4 x D-30KP turbofans
Thrust:	12,025kg (26,455lb) each
Maximum Speed:	850km/h (528mph)
Ceiling:	10,200m (33,465ft)
Range:	7300km (4536 miles)
Armament:	wingtip ECM pods and self-defence flares
Systems:	Schnel-M airborne radar and guidance system, NPK-T flight control and navigation system
Date Deployed:	1984

AN-70

Without the break-up of the former Soviet Union, the An-70, which was designed to meet the needs of the air force's transport needs, would probably be already in service today. However, the programme got caught up in the chaos generated by the political changes in Russia which propelled the formerly centrally controlled aerospace industry into a serious crisis. The An-70 heavy transport is a replacement for the An-12 "Cub". The first flight was on 16 December 1994. It has the same high wing and tail loading ramp that are typical among tactical freight aircraft, but a novelty is the use of contra-rotating propfans (with six and eight blades). The landing gear permits the An-70 to operate from unpaved airfields, and expected airframe life is 20,000 flights (45,000 flight hours, 25 years' service). The aircraft is equipped with a highly computerized control system, allowing quick diagnostics and service. The navigator's position is eliminated, with his functions and equipment transferred to the first officer's station. The flight engineer and radio operator stations are also eliminated. The pressurized cargo cabin has a temperature regulator and is equipped with in-floor cargo handling system, which makes the An-70 a self-sufficient aircraft that has no need for ground handling equipment. Production estimates are unknown.

SPECIFICATIONS

Primary Role:	transport
Crew:	3
Contractor:	Antonov
Length:	40.25m (132ft)
Wingspan:	44.06m (144.5ft)
Height:	16.1m (52.8ft)
Maximum Take-off Weight:	130,000kg (286,000lb)
Powerplant:	4 x ZMKB Ivchenko Progress D-27 propfans
Thrust:	unknown
Maximum Speed:	750km/h (469mph)
Ceiling:	9600m (31,496ft)
Range:	7250km (4531 miles)
Armament:	none
Systems:	unknown
Date Deployed:	unknown

AN-72 COALER

The An-72 Coaler is designed as a short take-off and landing (STOL) aircraft which can operate from unprepared airfields. The first prototype flew on 22 December 1977. The wings are high-mounted and back-tapered, with two turbofans mounted in long pods mounted on top of the wings. Round air intakes extend from the front of the wings' leading edges. The engines were placed on the leading edge of the wings to increase lift for STOL capability, with the jet exhausts blowing over titanium panels on the upper surface. The fuselage is circular with a round, solid nose, upswept rear section and a flush cockpit. The rear fuselage has a hinged loading ramp with a rear fairing that slides backwards and up to clear the opening. Loads can be air dropped, and there are folding side seats for 42 para-troops or 52 passengers. The An-72P is a maritime patrol variant with bulged observation windows, life raft provision and cameras as well as offensive armament, including under-wing rocket pods, a podded cannon on the undercarriage sponson and bombs that can be mounted in the rear fuselage and dropped through the open rear ramp. The An-74 deriva-tive features improved avionics, radar and increased range. It was designed to operate in the polar regions where it can land on ice floes for re-supply or rescue work.

SPECIFICATIONS

Primary Role:	*light STOL transport*
Crew:	*3*
Contractor:	*Antonov*
Length:	*28.1m (92ft)*
Wingspan:	*31.9m (104.5ft)*
Height:	*8.6m (28.3ft)*
Maximum Take-off Weight:	*34,500kg (76,060lb)*
Powerplant:	*2 x ZKMB Progress D-36 turbofans*
Thrust:	*13,027kg (28,660lb) each*
Maximum Speed:	*705km/h (438mph)*
Ceiling:	*11,800m (38,713ft)*
Range:	*4800km (3000 miles)*
Armament:	*none*
Systems:	*integrated flight control system*
Date Deployed:	*1979*

AN-124 CONDOR

The An-124 *Ruslan* is the world's largest and highest flying cargo capacity aircraft in production. The aircraft, which has the NATO reporting name Condor, is designed for long-range delivery and air dropping of heavy and large-size cargo, including machines, equipment and troops. The unique transport capabilities and high performance of the aircraft have been proven in operation. Examples include 91-tonne (90-ton) hydraulic turbines, large-size Liebherr autocranes, American Euclid dump trucks, the fuselage of a Tu-204 passenger transporter, a 111-tonne (109-ton) railway locomotive, and a sea yacht of more than 25m (82ft) in length. The aircraft fuselage has a double-deck layout. The cockpit, the relief crew compartment and the troop cabin with 88 seats are on the upper deck. The lower deck is the cargo hold. The flight deck has crew stations arranged in pairs for the six crew members: pilot and co-pilot, two flight engineers, the navigator and communications officer. The loadmaster's station is located in the lobby deck. The An-124 has a swept-back supercritical wing to give high aerodynamic efficiency and consequently a long flight range. The construction includes extruded skin panels on the wing, extruded plates for the centre-section wing panels and monolithic wafer plates for the fuselage panels.

SPECIFICATIONS

Primary Role:	*heavy transport*
Crew:	*6*
Contractor:	*Antonov*
Length:	*69.1m (226.6ft)*
Wingspan:	*73.3m (240.6ft)*
Height:	*20.8m (68.1ft)*
Maximum Take-off Weight:	*405,000kg (891,000lb)*
Powerplant:	*4 x Lotarev D18T turbofans*
Thrust:	*23,477kg (51,650lb) each*
Maximum Speed:	*865km/h (537mph)*
Ceiling:	*12,000m (39,370ft)*
Range:	*13,300km (8312 miles)*
Armament:	*none*
Systems:	*integrated flight control and aiming-navigation system*
Date Deployed:	*1984*

IL-76 CANDID

The Il-76 is a medium-range military transport aircraft known by the NATO codename Candid. The mission of the aircraft is to drop paratroopers; carry ground forces; combat materials with crews and armaments including medium-sized battle tanks; and also transport materials for disaster relief operations. The Il-76 is produced by the Ilyushin Aviation Company in Moscow and the Tashkent Aircraft Production Corporation in Tashkent, Uzbekistan. There are several design variants including the basic Il-76, Il-76M, Il-76MD and the Il-76-MF. In terms of design, aerodynamic configuration and flight performance characteristics, the Il-76M version virtually resembles the basic Il-76 aircraft, but has almost double the payload capacity. The aircraft is of a conventional aerodynamic configuration with a high-set swept wing and T-shaped tail unit. The crew cabin, cargo hold and rear compartment are fully pressurized. The beam-type fuselage has an oval section over the crew cabin and circular section over the cargo hold. The wing leading and trailing edges are fitted with highlift devices comprising deflectable five-section leading-edge slats, triple-slotted trailing-edge extension flaps, ailerons, spoilers and air brakes. The Il-76 is the true workhorse of the Russian aviation transport fleet.

SPECIFICATIONS

Primary Role:	medium transport
Crew:	6
Contractor:	Ilyushin
Length:	46.6m (152.8ft)
Wingspan:	50.5m (165.6ft)
Height:	14.7m (48.22ft)
Maximum Take-off Weight:	170,000kg (374,000lb)
Powerplant:	4 x Soloviev D-30KP turbofans
Thrust:	12,025kg (26,455lb) each
Maximum Speed:	850km/h (528mph)
Ceiling:	10,500m (34,448ft)
Range:	7300km (4562 miles)
Armament:	2 x 23mm GSh-23L cannons in the tail
Systems:	integrated flight control and aiming-navigation system
Date Deployed:	1974

IL-78 MIDAS

The Il-78 Midas aerial refuelling tanker is based on (or converted from) the airframe of the Il-76MD freighter, carrying a maximum payload of 48,000kg (105,600lb). When deployed in the early 1980s, it supported tactical and strategic aircraft and significantly improved the ability of Soviet aircraft to conduct longer-range operations. The former Soviet Union's only operational Il-78M regiment was based in the Ukraine, which retained the aircraft after independence. Only a handful remained in Russian hands. A three-point UPAZ-1A Sakhalin refuelling system allows it to serve one heavy bomber from the ventral point or two aircraft (MiG-31 or Su-24) simultaneously from the wing-mount points. The refuelling process is monitored by an operator occupying the gunner's position. His workplace is equipped with an optical rear view system, in addition to a radio and light signal equipment. Once connected, refuelled aircraft can receive fuel from the wing tanks at rate 900 to 2200 litres per minute. While early production Il-78s had removable fuselage tanks and could be used as military transports, the later, improved version Il-78M cannot be converted to a transporter. Midas entered service in 1987, replacing the outdated M-4 tankers that had served since the 1960s.

SPECIFICATIONS

Primary Role:	airborne tanker
Crew:	6
Contractor:	Ilyushin
Length:	46.6m (152.8ft)
Wingspan:	50.5m (165.6ft)
Height:	14.7m (48.4ft)
Maximum Take-off Weight:	210,000kg (462,000lb)
Powerplant:	4 x Soloviev D-30KP turbofans
Thrust:	12,025kg (26,455lb) each
Maximum Speed:	850km/h (528mph)
Ceiling:	10,500m (34,448ft)
Range:	2500km (1562 miles)
Armament:	2 x 23mm GSh-23L cannons in the tail
Systems:	integrated flight control and aiming-navigation system
Date Deployed:	1987

MIG-29 FULCRUM

The mission of the MiG-29 is to destroy hostile air targets within radar coverage limits and also to destroy ground targets using unguided weapons in visual flight conditions. The aircraft's fixed-wing profile with large-wing leading-edge root extensions gives good manoeuvrability and control at subsonic speed, including manoeuvres at high angles of attack. It is equipped with seven external weapon hardpoints. The aircraft can carry up to two R-27 air-to-air medium-range missiles; six R-73 and R-60 air-to-air short-range missiles; four pods of S-5, S-8 and S-24 unguided rockets; air bombs weighing up to 3000kg (6600lb); and a 30mm built-in aircraft gun with 150 rounds of ammunition. The aircraft is equipped with an information and fire control radar system comprising an N-019 radar developed by Phazotron Research and Production Company, Moscow; an infrared search and track sensor; a laser rangefinder; and a helmet-mounted target designator. The Russian Air Force has begun an upgrade programme for 150 of its MiG-29 fighters, which will be designated MiG-29SMT. The upgrade comprises increased range and payload, new glass cockpit, new avionics, improved radar, and an inflight refuelling probe. The radar will be the Phazotron Zhuk, capable of tracking 10 targets to a maximum range of 245km (153 miles).

SPECIFICATIONS

Primary Role:	*fighter*
Crew:	*1*
Contractor:	*Moscow Air Production Organization*
Length:	*14.87m (48.75ft)*
Wingspan:	*11.36m (37.25ft)*
Height:	*4.73m (15.5ft)*
Maximum Take-off Weight:	*18,500kg (40,785lb)*
Powerplant:	*2 x RD-33 turbofans*
Thrust:	*8300kg (18,260lb) each*
Maximum Speed:	*2400km/hr (1500mph)*
Ceiling:	*18,000m (59,055ft)*
Range:	*1500km (937 miles)*
Armament:	*AA-10, AA-11 & AA-8 AAMs, 1 x 30mm gun, bombs*
Systems:	*Slot Back radar, IRST, RWR, ballistic bombsight*
Date Deployed:	*1983*

SU-24 FENCER

The Su-24 Fencer is designed to penetrate hostile territory and destroy ground and surface targets in any weather conditions, by day and night. Variants of the Su-24 have also been produced for reconnaissance and electronic countermeasures duties. The aircraft has a conventional aerodynamic configuration with a variable-sweep shoulder wing. The fuselage is of rectangular section semi-monocoque design with a two-seat pressurized cockpit. The wing sweep-back angle varies from 16 to 69 degrees with respect to the wing leading edge. The tail unit comprises all-moving horizontal tail surfaces and a single-fin vertical tail fitted with a rudder. The horizontal tail surfaces function as elevators when deflecting symmetrically and as ailerons when deflecting differentially, and a tricycle-type landing gear allows the aircraft to be operated from either concrete or unpaved runways. The Su-24M entered service in 1983 and is a development of the Su-24. Over 900 Su-24s have been delivered and the aircraft is in service with the Russian Air Force and Navy and the air forces of Azerbaijan, Algeria, Iran, Libya, Poland, Syria and the Ukraine. As well as bombs and missiles, the aircraft can carry up to three gun pods with 23mm Gsh-6-23 guns, which have a rate of fire of 9000 rounds per minute and fire unit of 500 rounds.

SPECIFICATIONS

Primary Role:	*tactical bomber*
Crew:	*2*
Contractor:	*Sukhoi*
Length:	*24.53m (80.5ft)*
Wingspan:	*17.63m (57.8ft) to10.36m (34ft)*
Height:	*4.97m (16.25ft)*
Maximum Take-off Weight:	*39,700kg (87,520lb)*
Powerplant:	*2 x AL-21F-3A turbojets*
Thrust:	*22,454kg (49,400lb) each*
Maximum Speed:	*1550km/hr (969mph)*
Ceiling:	*11,000m (36,089ft)*
Range:	*2100km (1312 miles)*
Armament:	*1 x 23mm six-barrelled cannon, AS-7, AS-10, AS-11, AS-12, AS-13, AS-14 AGMs*
Systems:	*PNS-24 integrated navigation and aiming system*
Date Deployed:	*1983*

SU-25 FROGFOOT

The Su-25 is designed to defeat small mobile and stationary ground targets and to engage low-speed air targets. A two-seat variant, the Su-35UB (Frogfoot-B), is a weapons training aircraft manufactured at Ulan-Ude. The Su-25UTG is the two-seater aircraft carrier variant fitted with an arrester hook under the tail. The Su-25UTG is deployed on the Russian Navy aircraft carrier *Admiral Kuznetsov*. An upgraded Su-25K, the Scorpion, has been developed by Tbilisi Aerospace Manufacturing (TAM) of Georgia with Elbit of Israel. Scorpion has a new advanced avionics system with a weapons delivery and navigation system for both NATO and Eastern European weapons and pods, and new glass cockpit with two multi-colour LCD displays and head-up display (HUD). The aircraft's twin-barrel gun, the 30mm AO-17A, is installed in the underside of the fuselage on the port side. The gun is armed with 250 rounds of ammunition and is capable of firing at a burst rate of 3000 rounds per minute. SPPU-22 gun pods can also be installed on the underwing pylons. The pods carry the GSh-23 23mm twin-barrel guns, each with 260 rounds of ammunition. The aircraft is equipped with self-sealing foam-filled fuel tanks, and its range can be extended by the provision of four PTB-1500 external fuel tanks.

SPECIFICATIONS

Primary Role:	*close support*
Crew:	*1*
Contractor:	*Sukhoi*
Length:	*15.53m (50.9ft)*
Wingspan:	*14.36m (47ft)*
Height:	*4.8m (15.75ft)*
Maximum Take-off Weight:	*17,600kg (38,800lb)*
Powerplant:	*2 x R-195 turbojets*
Thrust:	*9019kg (19,842lb) each*
Maximum Speed:	*975km/h (606mph)*
Ceiling:	*7000m (22,966ft)*
Range:	*1250km (781 miles)*
Armament:	*1 x twin 30mm cannon, AA-8, AA-10 AAMs; AS-7, AS-10, AS-14 AGMs*
Systems:	*Klyon PS target designator, Gardeniya radar jammer*
Date Deployed:	*1981*

SU-27 FLANKER

Designed as a high-performance fighter with a fly-by-wire control system, the highly manoeuvrable Su-27 is one of the most imposing fighters ever built. The first "Flanker-A'" prototype flew on 20 May 1977 and entered service as the "Flanker-B" in 1984. The development of the Su-27 fighter was completed in the early 1980s, and the aircraft subsequently set more than 40 world records of altitude and take-off speed. It was the forerunner of an entire family of fighter aircraft, including the Su-27UB training variant, the Su-33 carrier-based fighter, the Su-37 multi-mission aircraft and the Su-32FN two-seat specialized version. The Su-27UB is a two-seat training version of the Su-27 which first flew in March 1985. The aircraft is equipped to operate autonomously in combat over hostile territory, as an escort to deep-penetration strike aircraft, and in the suppression of enemy airfields. The Flanker also provides general air defence in cooperation with ground and airborne control stations. The Su-27 is in service with Russia, Ukraine, Belarus, Kazakhstan and Vietnam, and is built under licence in China, where it is designated the F-11. A variant, the Su-30MK, has also been sold to India where licensed local production began in 2000. There is no doubt that Flanker is one of the most potent warplanes in service.

SPECIFICATIONS

Primary Role:	*interceptor*
Crew:	*1*
Contractor:	*Sukhoi*
Length:	*21.935m (71.9ft)*
Wingspan:	*14.7m (48.2ft)*
Height:	*5.932m (19.5ft)*
Maximum Take-off Weight:	*22,000kg (48,400lb)*
Powerplant:	*2 x Lyulka AL-31F turbofans*
Thrust:	*25,052kg (55,114lb) each*
Maximum Speed:	*2500km/h (1562mph)*
Ceiling:	*18,500m (60695ft)*
Range:	*4000km (2500 miles)*
Armament:	*1 x 30mm cannon, AA-8, AA-9, AA-10, AA-11, AAMs*
Systems:	*Pulse Doppler radar, fly-by-wire system*
Date Deployed:	*1984*

SU-27P FLANKER

Largely based on the Su-27UB two-seat trainer, the Su-27P has a new radio location system which can transmit the positions of 10 targets to four other fighters at the same time. The Su-27P (also called the Su-30) is made at Irkutsk. Due to development difficulties, work on the two-seat version had to be set aside until the single-seat version was in production, and the first two-seat T10U prototype did not fly until March 1985, entering production and service as the Sukhoi Su-27UB two years later. The Su-27UB has a tandem-seat arrangement under a single canopy, with the back seat stepped up above the front seat, providing the flight instructor in the back seat a good view in front of the aircraft and of what the trainee in the front seat is doing. This arrangement gives the Su-27UB an even more "crane-necked" appearance than the Su-27. The Su-27UB was designed to be fully combat capable, and the second seat was accommodated by stretching the fuselage. The vertical tail-fins were increased in height slightly to compensate for the changed aerodynamics. The addition of the second seat increased the weight of the aircraft by only about 1120kg (2470lb) without reduction in fuel capacity, and aside from minor decreases in top speed, the Su-27P's performance is very similar to that of the single-seat Su-27.

SPECIFICATIONS

Primary Role:	long-range intercept fighter
Crew:	2
Contractor:	Sukhoi
Length:	21.94m (71.98ft)
Wingspan:	14.70m (48.22ft)
Height:	6.36m (20.86ft)
Maximum Take-off Weight:	34,000kg (74,800lb)
Powerplant:	2 x Lyulka AL-31 turbofans
Thrust:	25,051kg (55,114lb) each
Maximum Speed:	2125km/h (1328mph)
Ceiling:	17,500m (57,414ft)
Range:	5200km (3250 miles)
Armament:	1 x 30mm gun, AA-10, AA-11, AA-12 AAMs, bombs
Systems:	Phazotron N001 Zhuk pulse Doppler radar, OEPS-27 electro-optic system, fly-by-wire system
Date Deployed:	1987

TU-95 BEAR

Development of the Tu-95 Bear bomber began in the early 1950s after series production of the medium-range Tu-4 started. The Bear's wings are mid-mounted, swept-back and tapered with blunt tips, and the engine nacelles extend well beyond the wings' leading edges. The fuselage of the Bear is tube-shaped with a rounded nose that tapers to the rear. It also has a stepped cockpit and a tail gun compartment. The tail of the aircraft is a fin that is swept-back and tapered with a square tip. There have been many variants, the most modern being the Bear H, the Tu-95MS. This entirely new variant became the launch platform for the long-range Kh-55 (AS-15) air-launched cruise missile. The initial version carried the missiles located in the bomb bay on a catapult. This was the first new production of a strike version of the Bear airframe since the 1960s. With the Bear H in series production, the decline in the inventory of Bear aircraft was reversed. The version designated as Tu-95MS6 aircraft carried Kh-55s located in the bomb bay on a rotary launcher. The Tu-95MS16 carried six missiles inside the fuselage and 10 missiles underneath the wings. Three underwing pylons are fitted under each inner wing panel. The Bear will remain in service until 2015, Russia's fragile finances permitting.

SPECIFICATIONS

Primary Role:	strategic bomber
Crew:	7
Contractor:	Tupolev
Length:	49.6m (162.7ft)
Wingspan:	51.1m (167.6ft)
Height:	13.4m (44ft)
Maximum Take-off Weight:	185,000kg (407,000lb)
Powerplant:	4 x NK-12MV turboprops
Thrust:	6818kg (15,000lb) each
Maximum Speed:	830km/h (519mph)
Ceiling:	12,000m (39,370ft)
Range:	10,500km (6562 miles)
Armament:	2 x 23mm guns, 16 x Kh-55
Systems:	Clam Pipe nav/bombing radar, Box Tail gun fire control radar, ECM, Ground Bouncer ECM jamming system, RWR
Date Deployed:	1981 (Bear H)

TU-160 BLACKJACK

The Tu-160 is a multi-mission strategic bomber designed for operations ranging from subsonic speeds and low altitudes to speeds over Mach 1 at high altitudes. The two weapons bays can accommodate different mission-specific loads, including strategic cruise missiles, short-range guided missiles, nuclear and conventional bombs, and mines. Its basic armament of short-range guided missiles and strategic cruise missiles enables it to deliver nuclear strikes against targets with pre-assigned coordinates. The Tu-160 was the outcome of a multi-mission bomber competition, which included a Tupolev proposal for an aircraft design using elements of the Tu-144, the Myasishchev M-18, and a Sukhoi design based on the T-4 aircraft. The project of Myasishchev was considered to be the most successful, although the Tupolev organization was regarded as having the greatest potential for completing this complex project. Consequently, Tupolev was assigned to develop an aircraft using elements of the Myasishchev M-18 bomber design. The project was supervised by V.N. Binznyuk. Trial operations in the air force began in 1987 with serial production being conducted at the Kazan Aviation Association. The Blackjack programme has encountered severe financial problems, and its future is uncertain.

SPECIFICATIONS

Primary Role:	strategic bomber
Crew:	4
Contractor:	Tupolev
Length:	54.1m (177.5ft)
Wingspan:	55.7m (182.75ft) to 50.7m (166.3ft)
Height:	13.1m (43ft)
Maximum Take-off Weight:	275,000kg (606,260lb)
Powerplant:	4 x MK-321 turbofans
Thrust:	25,000kg (55,000lb) each
Maximum Speed:	2000km/h (1250mph)
Ceiling:	16,000m (52,493ft)
Range:	12,300km (7687 miles)
Armament:	12 AS-16 SRAMs, 6 Kh-55 cruise missiles, nuclear weapons
Systems:	RID combined navigation-and-weapon aiming system, radio-electronic warfare systems
Date Deployed:	1987

YAK-141 FREESTYLE

The Yak-141 (formerly Yak-41) was originally intended to replace the Yak-38 for air defence of Kiev class carriers/cruisers, with secondary attack capabilities. Designed for carrier-borne operations as an air interceptor, close air combat, maritime and ground-attack, the Yak-141 has the same multi-mode radar as the MiG-29, although with a slightly smaller antenna housed in the nose radome. It features a triplex full authority digital fly-by-wire system. The Yak-141 continues previous Soviet V/STOL principles: combining a lift and propulsion jet with two fuselage-mounted lift jets in tandem behind the cockpit, with cruise power provided by a single Tumansky R-79 jet engine. The R-79 has a rear lift/cruise nozzle which deflects down for take-off, while the two lift engines have corresponding rearward vector to ensure stability. The airframe makes extensive use of composite materials, with some 28 percent of the airframe constructed of carbon-fibre, primarily in the tail assembly, while the remainder of the structure is mainly aluminum lithium alloys. The project began in 1975, but was delayed by financial constraints as well as the protracted development of the engine, which meant the prototype did not fly until March 1989. Four prototypes were built, two continuing in flight testing until 1995.

SPECIFICATIONS

Primary Role:	air defence
Crew:	1
Contractor:	Yakovlev
Length:	18.36m (60.2ft)
Wingspan:	10.105m (33.1ft) to 5.9m (19.3ft)
Height:	5m (16.3ft)
Maximum Take-off Weight:	19,500kg (42,900lb)
Powerplant:	1 x R-79-300 turbofan, 2 x Rybinsk RD- 41 turbofans
Thrust:	15,500kg (34,100lb)
Maximum Speed:	1250km/hr (781mph)
Ceiling:	15,000m (49,000ft)
Range:	2100km (1312 miles)
Armament:	1 x 30mm cannon, AA-10 AAMs, bombs, rockets
Systems:	multi-mode radar, HUD, OR-69 Sirena 3 RWR, ECM systems
Date Deployed:	unknown

C-212 AVIOCAR

The C-212 Aviocar 100 has a metal structure with a fixed tricycle landing gear and propellers with a variable and reversible pitch. Being a short take-off and landing (STOL) aircraft, it can use short runways. The C-212 is CASA's answer to the needs of different air forces in the field of light military transport and can operate in areas lacking in infrastructure and from unpaved runways. The C-212 was designed with simple and reliable systems. The wings are high-mounted and unequally tapered from mid-wing to the square tips. Two turboprop engines are mounted in pods under the wings' leading edges. The thick, cigar-shaped fuselage has a flat bottom and upswept rear section, with a stepped cockpit. The fuselage comprises two areas: the cockpit and the cargo compartment. The cargo compartment can carry 18 passengers and their luggage, or 16 parachutists fully equiped, or 2000kg (4400lb) of cargo, including road vehicles. For medical evacuations, 12 stretches and two seats can be mounted. Its cabin, open along the whole of the length of the plane, is complemented by the rear ramp which enables different logistic transport tasks to be carried out. The rear ramp can be opened while on the ground to load and unload; or in flight, for the launching of cargo, survival equipment or paratroopers.

SPECIFICATIONS

Primary Role:	STOL, light utility transport
Crew:	2
Contractor:	CASA
Length:	15.18m (49.75ft)
Wingspan:	19.12m (62.3ft)
Height:	6.29m (20.63ft)
Maximum Take-off Weight:	8100kg (17,820lb)
Powerplant:	2 x TPE331-10R-513C turboprops
Thrust:	1342kg (2952lb) each
Maximum Speed:	370km/h (231mph)
Ceiling:	9900m (32,480ft)
Range:	2680km (1675 miles)
Armament:	none
Systems:	electronic flight instruments system (EFIS), ESM, ECM, ELINT, COMINT
Date Deployed:	1972

JA 37 VIGGEN

In December 1961, the Swedish government approved the development of Aircraft System 37, the Viggen. The basic platform was the AJ 37 attack aircraft, to be followed by the S 37 reconnaissance version and JA 37 fighter. The new aircraft had a novel and advanced aerodynamic configuration to meet the short take-off and landing (STOL) and other performance requirements demanded of Swedish military aircraft: a fixed foreplane with flaps was mounted ahead of and slightly above the delta main wing. On 8 February 1967 the first prototype of the Saab 37 Viggen family made its maiden flight. In April 1968, the government authorized Viggen production and the first aircraft was delivered to the air force in July 1971. A total of 329 aircraft were eventually built in attack, trainer, two reconnaissance versions and the more powerful fighter variant that included new avionics, new air-to-air missiles (AAMs) and Europe's first pulse doppler radar. The last of 329 Viggens, a JA 37 fighter version, was delivered from Saab in Linköping to the Swedish Air Force in 1990. Since then, the Viggen has undergone several upgrades, the latest being Model D for the fighter version, which includes communication and weapon systems similar to those found in the Gripen. The Viggen has served the air force well for over 30 years.

SPECIFICATIONS

Primary Role:	*multirole fighter*
Crew:	*1*
Contractor:	*Saab*
Length:	*15.58m (51.1ft)*
Wingspan:	*10.6m (34.75ft)*
Height:	*5.9m (19.3ft)*
Maximum Take-off Weight:	*17,000kg (37,478lb)*
Powerplant:	*1 x Flygmotor RM8B turbofan*
Thrust:	*12,776kg (28,108lb)*
Maximum Speed:	*2250km/h (1406mph)*
Ceiling:	*18,300m (60,00ft)*
Range:	*2000km (1250 miles)*
Armament:	*1 x 30mm cannon, RB71, RB74 AAMs; bombs; RBS 15F anti-ship missile,*
Systems:	*ECM, countermeasures pod, ECCM*
Date Deployed:	*1971*

JAS39 GRIPEN

The Gripen fighter combines new avionics systems, modern materials, advanced aerodynamic design, a well-proven engine and fully integrated system to produce a highly capable, true multirole combat aircraft. The Gripen is the first Swedish aircraft that can be used for interception, ground-attack and reconnaissance (hence the Swedish abbreviation JAS – Fighter (J), Attack (A) and Reconnaissance (S) in Swedish) and is now successively replacing the Draken and Viggen. Gripen offers high agility, advanced target acquisition systems, low environmental signatures and a comprehensive electronic warfare (EW) suite. Currently, the Gripens used by the Swedish Air Force are armed with AIM-120 AMRAAM, AIM-9 Sidewinder, the Saab Dynamics RBS 15F for ship targets, and the Maverick ground-attack missile. A total of 204 aircraft in three batches have been ordered for the Swedish Air Force; the first batch of 30 aircraft has been completed. Deliveries from the second batch are ongoing, and comprise 96 one-seater and 14 two-seater aircraft. About 60 Gripens are in service with the Swedish Air Force. In June 1997, a third batch of 64 Gripens was approved by the Swedish government. This will take the total for the Swedish Air Force to 204. Production of batch three is scheduled for between 2002 and 2007.

SPECIFICATIONS

Primary Role:	multirole combat aircraft
Crew:	1
Contractor:	SAAB, Ericsson, Volvo, FFV Aerotech
Length:	14.1m (46.25ft)
Wingspan:	8.4m (27.5ft)
Height:	4.5 m (14.75ft)
Maximum Take-off Weight:	12,500kg (27,500lb)
Powerplant:	1 x Volvo Aero RM 12
Thrust:	8182kg (18,000lb)
Maximum Speed:	2450km/h (1531mph)
Ceiling:	14,021m (46,000ft)
Range:	unknown
Armament:	1 x 27mm gun, AMRAAM, Sidewinder, SRAAM AAMs, RBS 15F ASM
Systems:	pulse doppler radar, FLIR, infrared search and track
Date Deployed:	1997

S100B ARGUS

The Saab 340 is a Swedish twin-engined turboprop aircraft. An airborne early warning (AEW) version with a phased-array radar in a rectangular pod on top of the fuselage was developed in the early 1990s. In 1994 the first Saab 340 AEW & C was produced, and a year later it was re-designated S100B (S – *Spaning* – Reconnaissance) and given the official name Argus. The Swedish Air Force ordered six aircraft, four of which will be fitted with radar. Some are used by Japan as search and rescue aircraft. The Ericsson PS-890 Erieye radar uses an active array with 200 solid-state modules. Utilizing adaptive side lobe suppression, the look angle on each side is about 160 degrees. From its standard operational altitude of 6000m (19,685ft) the radar has a maximum range of 450km (279 miles). Against a fighter-sized target effective range is approximately 330km (205 miles). Seaborne targets can be detected at 320km (200 miles), though this is a function dependent on the aircraft's cruising height. The electronically scanned antenna can scan sectors of interest frequently while others are monitored, and a single sector can be scanned in different modes at the same time. The aircraft does not carry controllers (although it is large enough to do so), but functions as an airborne radar integrated with the total air defence network.

SPECIFICATIONS

Primary Role:	*airborne early warning*
Crew:	*2–5*
Contractor:	*Saab-Scania Aktiebolag, Aerospace Division*
Length:	*19.7m (64.6ft)*
Wingspan:	*21.4m (70.3ft)*
Height:	*6.9m (22.8ft)*
Maximum Take-off Weight:	*13,181kg (29,000lb)*
Powerplant:	*2 x General Electric CT7-9B turboprops*
Thrust:	*2600kg (5720lb) each*
Maximum Speed:	*463km/h (288mph)*
Ceiling:	*7620m (4762 miles)*
Range:	*1300km (812 miles)*
Armament:	*none*
Systems:	*Ericsson PS-890 Erieye radar*
Date Deployed:	*1994*

IDF

aiwan produced the *Ching-kuo* Indigenous Defence Fighter (IDF) with extensive assistance from American corporations, led by General Dynamics. With a combat radius of 960km (600 miles) while carrying out armed reconnaissance and patrol missions, the IDF is capable of conducting pre-emptive raids and strikes at airports along the Chinese coast. Its main role is one of air superiority, but it is also capable of carrying "Hsiung Feng-II" missiles to attack targets at sea. Most of the IDFs are expected to be armed with the indigenously produced BVR Tien Chien-II (Sky Sword-II) air-to-air missile (AAM). The IDF has faced numerous developmental and operational problems since its inception in the 1980s. Nevertheless, its technical sophistication, with its fly-by-wire controls and blended wing-body design, is believed to be superior to any aircraft produced and deployed by China to date. By 1997 some 60 had been built, and production of all 130 IDFs has now been completed. The twin-engine IDF is similar to the F-16 except that it is slightly smaller and has a slightly shorter range. The IDF is a hybrid as far as its external appearance is concerned. The nose of the fighter is a replica of the US F-20A Tigershark, while its body, wings and vertical tail surface are apparently lifted from the F-16.

SPECIFICATIONS

Primary Role:	*air superiority fighter*
Crew:	*1*
Contractor:	*AIDC*
Length:	*13.26m (43.5ft)*
Wingspan:	*9m (29.5ft)*
Height:	*4.04m (13.25ft)*
Maximum Take-off Weight:	*12,273kg (27,000lb)*
Powerplant:	*2 x ITEC (Garrett/AIDC) TFE1042-70 turbofans*
Thrust:	*4300kg (9460lb) each*
Maximum Speed:	*1275km/h (797mph)*
Ceiling:	*16,760m (54,987ft)*
Range:	*unknown*
Armament:	*1 x 20mm cannon;S ky Sword I and II AAMs; Hsiung Feng II ASM*
Systems:	*GD-53 pulse doppler radar, IRWR*
Date Deployed.	*1994*

A-4 SKYHAWK

The US Marine Corps' A-4 Skyhawk is a lightweight, single-engine attack aircraft. The mission of an A-4 squadron is to attack and destroy surface targets in support of the landing force commander, escort helicopters, and conduct other operations as directed. Developed in the early 1950s, the A-4 Skyhawk was originally designated the A-4D. It was a lightweight, daylight only, nuclear capable strike aircraft for use in large numbers from aircraft carriers. There are numerous models of the A-4 in use. The A-4M and the TA-4F (trainer) are currently used by Marine Corps Reserve squadrons. All models have two internally mounted 20mm cannons, and are capable of delivering conventional and nuclear weapons under day and night visual meteorological conditions. The A-4M uses a head-up display (HUD) and computer-aided delivery of its bomb load with the angle rate bombing system. The Marine Reserve has two squadrons of A-4s with 12 aircraft each. Additionally, each squadron has two TA-4 aircraft. The A-4 aircraft is one of the most effective and versatile light attack aircraft produced. Though the Skyhawk is over 30 years old, export models are still highly regarded and undergoing modern avionics, weapons and engine upgrades to maintain their flying prowess into the twenty-first century.

SPECIFICATIONS

Primary Role:	*attack aircraft*
Crew:	*1*
Contractor:	*McDonnell Douglas*
Length:	*12.98m (42.58ft)*
Wingspan:	*8.38m (27.5ft)*
Height:	*4.66m (15.25ft)*
Maximum Take-off Weight:	*11,113kg (24,500lb)*
Powerplant:	*1 x J-52-P-408A turbojet*
Thrust:	*5091kg (11,200lb)*
Maximum Speed:	*1052km/h (657mph)*
Ceiling:	*12,880m (42,257ft)*
Range:	*3225km (2016 miles)*
Armament:	*2 x 20mm cannon; Sidewinder, Shrike and Walleye missiles; AGM-65 Maverick ASM*
Systems:	*TACAN, IFF, HUD, AN/AVQ-24, AN/ASN-41*
Date Deployed:	*1962*

A-10 THUNDERBOLT

The A-10 and OA-10 Thunderbolt IIs were the first air force aircraft specially designed for close air support of ground forces. They are simple, effective and survivable twin-engine jet aircraft that can be used against all ground targets, their seven-barrelled Gatling gun being particularly potent. The primary mission of the A-10 is to provide day and night close air combat support for friendly land forces; its secondary mission is supporting search and rescue and Special Forces operations. Specific survivability features include a titanium armour-plated cockpit, redundant flight control system separated by fuel tanks, manual reversion mode for flight controls, foam-filled fuel tanks, ballistic foam void fillers, and a redundant primary structure providing "get home" capability after being hit. Design simplicity, ease of access and left-to-right interchangeable components make the A/OA-10 easily maintainable and suitable for deployment at advanced bases. It has excellent manoeuvrability at low air speeds and altitudes, and is a highly accurate weapons-delivery platform. Its wide combat radius and short take-off and landing (STOL) capability permit operations in and out of locations near frontlines. Using night vision goggles, Thunderbolt pilots can conduct their missions during darkness with ease.

SPECIFICATIONS

Primary Role:	close air support
Crew:	1
Contractor:	Fairchild Republic
Length:	16.16m (53ft)
Wingspan:	17.42m (57.15ft)
Height:	4.42m (14.5ft)
Maximum Take-off Weight:	22,950kg (51,000lb)
Powerplant:	2 x GE TF34-GE-100 turbofans
Thrust:	4120kg (9065lb) each
Maximum Speed:	672km/h (420mph)
Ceiling:	13,636m (45,000ft)
Range:	1280km (800 miles)
Armament:	1 x 30mm gun; Mk 82, Mk 84, CBU-52, CBU-58, CBU-71, CBU-87, CBU-89 bombs, AGM-65 Maverick ASM
Systems:	LASTE, GCAS
Date Deployed:	1976

AC-130H SPECTRE

The AC-130H Spectre gunship's primary missions are close air support, air interdiction and armed reconnaissance. These heavily armed aircraft incorporate side-firing weapons integrated with sophisticated sensor, navigation and fire-control systems to provide surgical firepower or area saturation during extended periods, at night and in adverse weather. The AC-130H is an excellent fire support platform with outstanding capabilities. With its extremely accurate fire-control system, it can place 105mm, 40mm and 25mm munitions on target with first-round accuracy. The new AC-130U Spectre gunship is being fielded as a replacement for the AC-130A aircraft. The AC-130U airframe is integrated with an armour protection system (APS), high-resolution sensors, infrared detection set (IDS), avionics and EW systems, and an armament suite consisting of side-firing, trainable 25mm, 40mm and 105mm guns. The AC-130U is the most complex aircraft weapon system in the world today: it has more than 609,000 lines of software code in its mission computers and avionics systems. The newest addition to the command fleet, it can provide surgical firepower or area saturation during extended loiter periods, against targets that include troops, fortifications and armoured vehicles.

SPECIFICATIONS

Primary Role:	*close air support*
Crew:	*14*
Contractor:	*Lockheed Aircraft Corporation*
Length:	*29.8m (97.75ft)*
Wingspan:	*40.4m (132.5ft)*
Height:	*11.7m (38.5ft)*
Maximum Take-off Weight:	*70,454kg (155,000lb)*
Powerplant:	*4 x T56-A-15 turboprops*
Thrust:	*6724kg (14,793lb) each*
Maximum Speed:	*480km/h (300mph)*
Ceiling:	*7576m (25,000ft)*
Range:	*2400km (1500 miles)*
Armament:	*2 x 20mm cannons, 1 x 40mm, 1 x 105mm*
Systems:	*DIRCM, AN/AAR-44 infrared warning receiver, AN/AAR-47 missile warning system*
Date Deployed:	*1972*

AV-8B HARRIER

The AV-8B V/STOL strike aircraft was designed to replace the AV-8A and the A-4M light attack aircraft. The Marine Corps had a requirement for a V/STOL light attack force since the late 1950s. Combining tactical mobility, responsiveness, reduced operating costs and flexibility, both afloat and ashore, V/STOL aircraft are particularly well-suited to the special combat and expeditionary requirements of the Marines. The AV-8BII+ features the APG-65 radar common to the F/A-18, as well as all previous systems and features common to the AV-8BII. The mission of the V/STOL squadron is to attack and destroy surface and air targets, to escort helicopters, and to conduct other such air operations as may be directed. It is operational with the US Marine Corps, the Spanish Navy and the Italian Navy. Weapons include the air-to-air AMRAAM and Sparrow missiles, air-to-surface AGM-65 Maverick missiles, and anti-ship Harpoon and Sea Eagle missiles, 25mm cannon and a range of bombs and rockets. The AGM-65 Maverick missile is installed on the Italian Harrier II Plus. The Harrier II Plus is also capable of deploying the Sea Eagle anti-ship missile, which is a fire-and-forget sea-skimming missile also carried on the Sea Harrier, and the air-launch version of the AGM 84 Harpoon surface strike missile.

SPECIFICATIONS

Primary Role:	*close air support, interceptor*
Crew:	*1*
Contractor:	*McDonnell Douglas*
Length:	*14.12m (46.3ft)*
Wingspan:	*9.25m (30.3ft)*
Height:	*3.55m (11.6ft)*
Maximum Take-off Weight:	*14,061kg (31,000lb)*
Powerplant:	*1 x Pegasus F402-RR-406 turbofan*
Thrust:	*10,091kg (22,200lb)*
Maximum Speed:	*1065km/h (666mph)*
Ceiling:	*15,000m (49,212ft)*
Range:	*2408km (1505 miles)*
Armament:	*1 x 25mm gun system, AGM-65, AIM-9L/M Sidewinder, GBU-12, GBU-16, CBU-99/100*
Systems:	*NAVFLIR, ARBS, AN/APG-65 radar system*
Date Deployed:	*1993*

B-1B LANCER

The B-1B is a multirole, long-range bomber capable of penetrating present and predicted sophisticated enemy defences. It can perform a variety of missions, including that of a conventional weapons carrier for theatre operations. The swing-wing design and turbofan engines not only provide greater range and high speed at low levels, they also enhance the bomber's overall survivability. Wing sweep at the full-forward position allows a short take-off and a fast base-escape profile for airfields under attack. Once airborne, the wings are positioned for maximum cruise distance or high-speed penetration. Differences between the B-1B and its predecessor, the B-1A of the 1970s, include a simplified engine inlet, modified over-wing fairing and relocated pilot tubes. The B-1B was structurally redesigned to increase its gross take-off weight from 179,545kg to 216,818kg (395,000lb to 477,000lb). This added take-off weight capacity, in addition to a moveable bulkhead between the forward and intermediate weapons bay, allows the B-1B Lancer to carry a wide variety of nuclear and conventional munitions. The most significant changes, however, are in the avionics, with an overall low-radar cross-section, automatic terrain-following high-speed penetration, and extremely precise weapons delivery.

SPECIFICATIONS

Primary Role:	*long-range bomber*
Crew:	*4*
Contractor:	*Rockwell, North American Aircraft*
Length:	*44.5m (146ft)*
Wingspan:	*41.8m (137ft) to 24.1m (79ft)*
Height:	*10.4m (34ft)*
Maximum Take-off Weight:	*216,818kg (477,000lb)*
Powerplant:	*4 x F-101-GE-102 turbofans*
Thrust:	*13,500kg (29,700lb) each*
Maximum Speed:	*1440km/h (900mph)*
Ceiling:	*9000m (30,000ft)*
Range:	*12,000km (7500 miles)*
Armament:	*8 x cruise missiles, freefall nuclear & conventional bombs*
Systems:	*JDAM, AN/ALQ 161A defensive avionics*
Date Deployed:	*1986*

B-2 SPIRIT

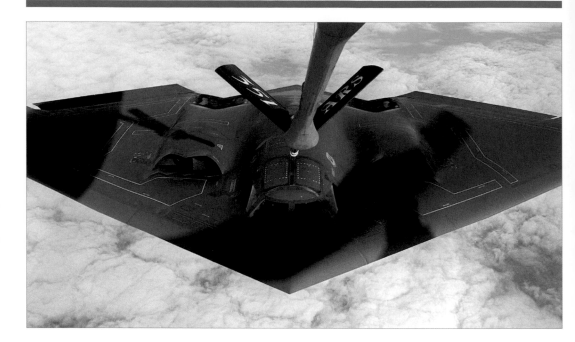

The B-2 programme was initiated in 1981, principally for strategic bombing missions against targets in Eastern Europe and Soviet Russia. With the fall of the Soviet Union, the emphasis of B-2 development was changed to conventional operations and the production number was reduced to 20 aircraft. The B-2's "stealth" characteristics give it the unique ability to penetrate an enemy's most sophisticated defences and threaten its most valued, heavily defended targets. The blending of low-observable technologies with high aerodynamic efficiency and large payload gives the B-2 important advantages over existing bombers. Its low observability gives it greater freedom of action at high altitudes, thus increasing its range and giving better field of view for the aircraft's sensors. Its low observability is derived from a combination of reduced infrared, acoustic, electromagnetic, visual and radar signatures. These signatures make it difficult for defensive systems to detect, track and engage the B-2. Many aspects of the low-observability manufacturing process remain classified; however, the Spirit's composite materials, special coatings and flying wing design all contribute to its "stealthiness". B-2s, in a conventional role, staging from Whiteman Air Force Base, Diego Garcia and Guam can cover the entire world with just one refuelling.

SPECIFICATIONS

Primary Role:	multirole heavy bomber
Crew:	2
Contractor:	Northrop Grumman
Length:	20.9m (69ft)
Wingspan:	52.12m (172ft)
Height:	5.1m (17ft)
Maximum Take-off Weight:	152,954kg (336,500lb)
Powerplant:	4 x F-118-GE-100 turbofans
Thrust:	7864kg (17,300lb) each
Maximum Speed:	classified
Ceiling:	15,240m (50,000ft)
Range:	12,223km (7639 miles)
Armament:	combination of 16 B61, B83, AGM–129 ACM, CBU-87, GBU-27, JDAM, TSSAM
Systems:	Line-of-Sight (LOS) data
Date Deployed:	1993

B-52 STRATOFORTRESS

The B-52H is the primary nuclear bomber in the USAF inventory. Only the H model is still in the air force inventory and all are assigned to the Air Combat Command. Starting in 1989, an on-going modification has incorporated the global positioning system, heavy stores adaptor beams for carrying 909kg (2000lb) munitions and additional smart weapons capability. In a conventional conflict, the B-52H can perform air interdiction, offensive counter-air and maritime operations. During Desert Storm, for example, B-52s delivered 40 percent of all the weapons dropped by Allied forces. It is highly effective when used for ocean surveillance, and can assist the US Navy in anti-ship and mine-laying operations. All aircraft are being modified to carry the AGM-142 Raptor missile and AGM-84 Harpoon anti-ship missile. There is a proposal under consideration to re-engine the remaining B-52H aircraft to extend their service life. If implemented, the B-52 will serve until 2025. However, the limiting factor of the B-52's service life is the economic limit of the aircraft's upper wing surface, calculated to have a life of 32,500 to 37,500 flight hours. Based on the projected economic service life and forecast mishap rates, the air force will be unable to maintain the requirement of 62 B-52 aircraft by 2044, after 84 years in service.

SPECIFICATIONS

Primary Role:	*heavy bomber*
Crew:	*5*
Contractor:	*Boeing*
Length:	*48.5m (159.1ft)*
Wingspan:	*56.4m (185ft)*
Height:	*12.4m (40.6ft)*
Maximum Take-off Weight:	*221,818kg (488,000lb)*
Powerplant:	*8 x TF33-P-3/103 turbofans*
Thrust:	*7650kg (17,000lb) each*
Maximum Speed:	*1040km/h (650mph)*
Ceiling:	*15,240m (50,000ft)*
Range:	*14,080km (8800 miles)*
Armament:	*27 internal weapons, 18 external weapons*
Systems:	*AN/ANS-136, AN/APN-224, AN/ASN-134, AN/APQ-156, AN/ASQ-175 AN/AYQ-10*
Date Deployed:	*1955*

C-2A GREYHOUND

The C-2A Greyhound twin-engine cargo aircraft was designed to land on aircraft carriers. In 1984 a contract was awarded for 39 new C-2A aircraft. Dubbed the Reprocured C-2A due to its similarity to the original, the new aircraft include substantial improvements in airframe and avionics systems. All the older C-2As were phased out in 1987, and the last of the new models was delivered in 1990. The avionics block upgrades for the C-2A(R) provide increased reliability and maintainability. A limited development test was conducted on the C-2A(R), due to the minor differences to the previous C-2A. Development test and evaluation and operational test and evaluation were performed by the Naval Air Warfare Center Aircraft Division from June 1985 to February 1986. These aircraft have a 4545kg (10,000lb) payload capacity and operate from forward area air stations in support of Atlantic and Pacific fleet operations. The aircraft's large aft door ramp and powered winch promote a fast turn-around time via straight-in rear loading and unloading. Special missions have been developed which employ the C-2A. These missions include personnel, combat rubber raiding craft (CRRC) and air cargo drops. The CRRC drops entail disembarking a team of divers and their equipment while airborne.

SPECIFICATIONS

Primary Role:	carrier cargo aircraft
Crew:	4
Contractor:	Grumann Aerospace
Length:	17.3m (57.75ft)
Wingspan:	24.69m (81ftt)
Height:	5m (17ft)
Maximum Take-off Weight:	25,909kg (57,000lb)
Powerplant:	2 x T-56-A-425 turboprops
Thrust:	7000kg (15,400lb) each
Maximum Speed:	563km/h (352mph)
Ceiling:	9100m (30,000ft)
Range:	2392km (1495 miles)
Armament:	none
Systems:	pulse doppler radar, two carrier approach systems
Date Deployed:	1965

C-5A/B GALAXY

The C-5 Galaxy is a heavy cargo transport designed to provide strategic airlift for the deployment and supply of combat and support forces. The C-5 can carry unusually large and heavy cargo over intercontinental ranges at jet speeds. Features unique to the C-5 include the forward cargo door and ramp and the aft cargo door system and ramp. These features allow drive-on/drive-off loading and unloading, as well as loading and unloading from either end of the cargo compartment. The C-5's kneeling capability also facilitates and expedites these operations by lowering cargo ramps for truck loading and reduces ramp angles for loading and unloading vehicles. The C-5's floor does not have tread-ways and the "floor-bearing pressure" is the same over the entire floor. The C-5A/B can carry up to 36 pallets. The troop compartment is located in the aircraft's upper deck. It is self-contained with a galley, two lavatories and 73 available passenger seats. Another 267 airline seats can be installed on the cargo compartment floor to give a maximum carrying capacity of 329 troops including air crew. At present, the C-5 has the highest operating cost of any military aircraft. For example, the A model requires 46 maintenance man hours per flying hour, with 16.7 maintenance man hours per flying hour for the B model.

SPECIFICATIONS

Primary Role:	*strategic airlift*
Crew:	*6*
Contractor:	*Lockheed-Georgia*
Length:	*75.3m (247ft)*
Wingspan:	*67.9m (222.75ft)*
Height:	*19.8m (65ft)*
Maximum Take-off Weight:	*381,818kg (840,000lb)*
Powerplant:	*4 x General Electric TF39-GE-1C turbofans*
Thrust:	*18,450kg (41,000lb) each*
Maximum Speed:	*866km/h (541mph)*
Ceiling:	*10,303m (34,000ft)*
Range:	*9504km (5940 miles)*
Armament:	*none*
Systems:	*Malfunction Detection Analysis and Recording System*
Date Deployed:	*1970*

C-17 GLOBEMASTER III

The C-17 Globemaster is capable of deploying troops and all types of cargo to main operating bases or directly to forward bases in the deployment area. The design of this cargo aircraft lets it operate on small, austere airfields. For example, the C-17 can take off and land on runways as short as 914m (3000ft) and as narrow as 27.4m (90ft) wide. Even on such narrow runways, the C-17 can turn around by using its backing capability while performing a three-point star turn. The manufacturers have made maximum use of off-the-shelf and commercial equipment, including air force standardized avionics. The design of the cargo compartment allows the C-17 to carry a wide range of vehicles, palleted cargo, paratroopers, airdrop loads and aeromedical evacuees. The cargo compartment has a sufficiently large cross-section to transport large wheeled and tracked vehicles, tanks, helicopters such as the AH-64 Apache, artillery and weapons such as the Patriot missile system. The C-17 is capable of carrying out an airdrop of outsized firepower such as the Sheridan light tank or Bradley fighting vehicle if the Bradley is refitted to be airdrop capable. Three Bradley armoured vehicles comprise one deployment load on the C-17. The US Army M-1 main battle tank can also be carried with other vehicles.

SPECIFICATIONS

Primary Role:	cargo and troop transport
Crew:	3
Contractor:	Boeing (McDonnell Douglas Corporation)
Length:	53.04m (173.9ft)
Wingspan:	51.81m (170.75ft)
Height:	16.79m (55ft)
Maximum Take-off Weight:	265,909kg (585,000lb)
Powerplant:	4 x Pratt & Whitney F117-PW-100 turbofans
Thrust:	18,590kg (40,900lb) each
Maximum Speed:	800km/h (500mph)
Ceiling:	13,716m (45,000ft)
Range:	unlimited with in-flight refuelling
Armament:	none
Systems:	AN/AAR-47 missile warning system
Date Deployed:	1993

C-20

The various versions of the C-20 are military modifications of the commercial Gulfstream aircraft. The C-20 aircraft provide distinguished visitor (DV) airlift for military and government officials, offering worldwide access while including a communications suite which supports worldwide secure voice and data communications for the DV and his staff. In June 1983 it was chosen as the replacement aircraft for the C-140B Jetstar, and three A models were delivered to the 89th Airlift Wing at Andrews Air Force Base under a cost-saving accelerated purchase plan. The three C-20As at Andrews were subsequently transferred to Ramstein Air Base, Germany. Seven B-model C-20s fly special air missions from Andrews. The primary difference between the C-20A and B models is the electrical system and avionics package. C-20B aircraft will reach their 20,000-hour service life in about 2014. The C-20D is a Gulfstream III aircraft capable of all-weather, long-range, high speed non-stop flights between airports. The C-20D aircraft are operated by Fleet Logistics Support Wing Detachment. The C-20G is a Gulfstream IV aircraft capable of all-weather, long-range, high speed flights between airports. They are operated by the Fleet Logistics Support Squadron Four Eight (VR-48) and the Marine Air Support Detachment (MASD).

SPECIFICATIONS

Primary Role:	operational support airlift, special air missions
Crew:	5
Contractor:	Gulfstream Aerospace
Length:	25.35m (83.16ft)
Wingspan:	23.71m (77.78in)
Height:	7.46m (24.5ft)
Maximum Take-off Weight:	31,682kg (69,700lb)
Powerplant:	2 x Rolls-Royce Spey MK511-8 turbofans
Thrust:	5182kg (11,400lb) each
Maximum Speed:	922km/h (576mph)
Ceiling:	13,715m (44,997ft)
Range:	7544km (4715 miles)
Armament:	none
Systems:	Honeywell Primus Avionics Suite
Date Deployed:	1983

C-130 HERCULES

The C-130 Hercules is capable of operating from rough airstrips and is the prime transport for paradropping troops and equipment into hostile areas. Basic and specialized versions perform a diversity of roles, including airlift support, DEW (Distant Early Warning) Line and Arctic ice re-supply, aeromedical missions, aerial spray missions, fire-fighting duties for the US Forest Service, and natural disaster relief missions. There are several variants: the initial production model was the C-130A; the C-130B introduced Allison T56-A-7 turboprops; and several A models, redesignated C-130D, were modified with wheel-ski landing gear for service in the Arctic. The C-130E is an extended-range development of the B, with two underwing fuel tanks and increased range and endurance capabilities. Similar to the E model, the C-130H has updated T56-A-T5 turboprops, a redesigned outer wing, updated avionics and other minor improvements. The the C-130J climbs faster and higher, flies farther at a higher cruise speed, and takes off and lands in a shorter distance. The C-130 can accommodate 92 combat troops or 64 fully equipped paratroopers on side-facing seats. For medical evacuations, it carries 74 litter patients and two medical attendants. Paratroopers exit the aircraft through two doors on either side of the aircraft or via the rear ramp.

SPECIFICATIONS

Primary Role:	transport
Crew:	5
Contractor:	Lockheed Martin
Length:	29.3m (97.75ft)
Wingspan:	39.7m (132.5ft)
Height:	11.4m (38.25ft)
Maximum Take-off Weight:	69,750kg (155,000lb)
Powerplant:	4 x T56-A-15 turboprops
Thrust:	6724kg (14,793lb) each
Maximum Speed:	598km/h (374mph)
Ceiling:	10,000m (33,000ft)
Range:	3770km (2356 miles)
Armament:	none
Systems:	GPS/INS, E-TCAS, SKE2000 station keeping system and an Instrument Landing System (ILS)
Date Deployed:	1955

C-141B STARLIFTER

The Starlifter can airlift combat forces, equipment and supplies, and deliver them on the ground or by air-drop, using paratrooper doors on each side and a rear loading ramp. It can be used for low-altitude delivery of paratroopers and equipment, and high-altitude delivery of paratroopers. It can also airdrop equipment and supplies using the container delivery system. It is the first aircraft designed to be compatible with the 463L Material Handling System, which permits the off-loading of 30,600kg (68,000lb) of cargo, refuelling and reloading a full load, all in less than an hour. The C-141 has an all-weather landing system, pressurized cabin and crew station. Its cargo compartment can easily be modified to perform around 30 different missions. About 200 troops or 155 fully equipped paratroopers can sit in canvas side-facing seats, or 166 troops in rear-facing airline seats. Rollers in the aircraft floor allow quick and easy cargo pallet loading. When palletized cargo is not being carried, the rollers can be turned over to leave a smooth, flat surface for the loading of vehicles. Several C-141s have been modified to carry the Minuteman missile in its special container, up to a total weight of 41,400kg (92,000lb). Some C-141s have intra-formation positioning for maintaining formation regardless of visibility.

SPECIFICATIONS

Primary Role:	*long-range transport*
Crew:	*6*
Contractor:	*Lockheed-Georgia*
Length:	*51m (168.3ft)*
Wingspan:	*48.5m (160ft)*
Height:	*11.9m (39.25ft)*
Maximum Take-off Weight:	*146,864kg (323,100lb)*
Powerplant:	*4 x Pratt & Whitney TF33-P-7 turbofans*
Thrust:	*9205kg (20,250lb) each*
Maximum Speed:	*800km/h (500mph)*
Ceiling:	*12,424m (41,000ft)*
Range:	*4000km (2500 miles)*
Armament:	*none*
Systems:	*Container Delivery System (CDS), 463L Material Handling System*
Date Deployed:	*1964*

E-2C HAWKEYE

The E-2C Hawkeye is the US Navy's all-weather, carrier-based tactical airborne warning and control system platform for the carrier battle group. Additional missions include surface surveillance coordination, strike and interceptor control, search and rescue guidance and communications relay. An integral component of the carrier air wing, the E-2C carries three primary sensors: radar, IFF and a passive detection system. These sensors are integrated through a general-purpose computer that enables the E-2C to provide early warning, threat analysis and control of counter action against air and surface targets. The E-2C incorporates the latest solid-state electronics. There is currently one squadron of four Hawkeyes in each carrier air wing. The large 7.3m- (24ft-) diameter circular antenna radome above the rear fuselage gives the E-2C its distinctive profile. The radome houses the AN/APA-171 antenna, which rotates at 5–6 revolutions per minute. The AN/APS-145 radar is capable of tracking more than 2000 targets and controlling the interception of 40 hostile targets. The radar's total radiation aperture-control antenna reduces sidelobes and is robust against electronic countermeasures (ECM). It is capable of detecting aircraft at ranges greater than 550 km (344 miles).

SPECIFICATIONS

Primary Role:	*carrier AEW aircraft*
Crew:	*5*
Contractor:	*Grumman*
Length:	*17.5m (57.41ft)*
Wingspan:	*24.6m (80.7ft)*
Height:	*5.6m (18.37ft)*
Maximum Take-off Weight:	*24,161kg (53,154lb)*
Powerplant:	*2 x T56-A-427 turboprops*
Thrust:	*7606kg (16,733lb) each*
Maximum Speed:	*626km/h (389mph)*
Ceiling:	*11,300m (37,073ft)*
Range:	*3000km (1875 miles)*
Armament:	*none*
Systems:	*AN/ASN-92 CAINS, AN/APS-145 radar, AN/UYQ-70 advanced display system*
Date Deployed:	*1973*

E-3 SENTRY

The E-3 Airborne Warning and Control System (AWACS) aircraft carries out airborne surveillance, and command, control and communications (C3) functions for both tactical and air defence forces. The E3 look-down radar has a 360-degree view of the horizon, and at operating altitudes has a range of more than 320km (200 miles). The radar can detect and track air and sea targets simultaneously. In a tactical role, the E-3 can detect and track hostile aircraft operating at low altitudes over any terrain, and can identify and control friendly aircraft in the same airspace. In the strategic defence role, the E-3 provides the means to detect, identify, track and intercept airborne threats. The basic E-3 is a militarized version of the Boeing 707-320B commercial jet airframe, distinguished by the addition of a large, rotating radome containing the main radar, identification friend or foe (IFF) and Tactical Data Information Link-Control (TADIL-C) antennas. The layout of the equipment in the fuselage is arranged in bays with areas allocated for communications, signal and data processing, command and control, navigation and target identification systems. The signal and data processing is carried out on a high-speed IBM 4PiCC-1 computer. The aircraft is equipped with 14 command and control consoles.

SPECIFICATIONS

Primary Role:	AWACS
Crew:	17
Contractor:	Boeing
Length:	46.62m (152.9ft)
Wingspan:	44.43m (145.75ft)
Height:	12.5m (41.75ft)
Maximum Take-off Weight:	151,955kg (335,000lb)
Powerplant:	4 x TF-33-PW-1 00 A turbofans
Thrust:	9545kg (21,000lb) each
Maximum Speed:	800km/h (500mph)
Ceiling:	10,670m (35,000ft)
Range:	9250km (5781 miles)
Armament:	none
Systems:	AN/APY-1/2 radar, Data Processing Functional Group, Tactical Data Information Link
Date Deployed:	1977

E-4B NAOC

The E-4B serves as the National Airborne Operations Center (NAOC) for the National Command Authorities. In cases of national emergency or destruction of ground command control centres, the aircraft provides a highly surviveable, command, control and communications centre to direct US forces, execute emergency war orders and coordinate actions by civil authorities. There are only four E-4B aircraft, with one constantly on alert. The E-4B, a militarized version of the Boeing 747-200, is a four-engine long-range, high-altitude aircraft capable of being refuelled in flight. The main deck is divided into six functional areas: a National Command Authorities' work area, conference room, briefing room, an operations team work area, communications area and rest areas. The E-4B has electromagnetic pulse protection, an electrical system designed to support advanced electronics and a wide variety of new communications equipment. Other improvements include nuclear and thermal effects shielding, acoustic control, an improved technical control facility and an upgraded air-conditioning system for cooling electrical components. An advanced satellite communications system also improves worldwide communications among strategic and tactical satellite systems and the airborne operations centre.

SPECIFICATIONS

Primary Role:	airborne operations centre
Crew:	up to 114
Contractor:	Boeing
Length:	70.5m (231.3ft)
Wingspan:	59.7m (195.6ft)
Height:	19.3m (63.5ft)
Maximum Take-off Weight:	360,000kg (800,000lb)
Powerplant:	4 x CF6-50E2 turbofans
Thrust:	23,863kg (52,500lb) each
Maximum Speed:	969km/h (602mph)
Ceiling:	9091m (30,000ft)
Range:	unknown
Armament:	none
Systems:	electromagnetic pulse protection, nuclear and thermal effects shielding, acoustic control
Date Deployed:	1980

E-6 MERCURY

The E-6 is the airborne portion of the TACAMO (take charge and move out) Communications System. It provides surviveable communication links between the National Command Authority (NCA) and strategic forces. The E-6 is a version of the commercial Boeing 707 aircraft: a long-range, air-refuelable aircraft equipped with four CFM-56-2A-2 high bypass ratio fan/jet engines with thrust reversers. The aircraft is electromagnetic pulse hardened. It has an endurance of over 15 hours without refuelling and a maximum endurance of 72 hours with inflight refuelling. The E-6B is a dual-mission aircraft capable of fulfiling either the E-6A mission or the airborne strategic command post mission and is equipped with an airborne launch control system (ALCS), which is capable of launching US land-based intercontinental ballistic missiles. The first E-6B aircraft was accepted in December 1997 and the E-6B assumed its dual operational mission in October 1998. The E-6 fleet will be completely modified to the E-6B configuration by 2003. In the TACAMO role, the E-6 flies independent random operations from various deployed sites for approximately 15-day intervals, and each deployed crew is self-supporting except for fuel and perishables. Mission commitment is in the Atlantic and Pacific regions.

SPECIFICATIONS

Primary Role:	airborne command post
Crew:	14
Contractor:	Boeing
Length:	45.8m (150.3ft)
Wingspan:	45.2m (148.3ft)
Height:	12.9m (42.5ft)
Maximum Take-off Weight:	155,000kg (341,000lb)
Powerplant:	4 x CFM-56-2A-2 high bypass turbofans
Thrust:	10,900kg (23,980lb) each
Maximum Speed:	960km/h (600mph)
Ceiling:	12,192m (40,000ft)
Range:	12,144km (7590 miles)
Armament:	none
Systems:	TACAMO suite, WING-TIP pods, trailing wire antenna, and four 75-KNA generators
Date Deployed:	1989

E-8C JOINT STARS

The Joint Surveillance Target Attack Radar System (Joint STARS) is a long-range, air-to-ground surveillance system designed to locate, classify and track ground targets in all weather conditions. It has a range of more than 250 km (150 miles). These capabilities make Joint STARS effective for dealing with any contingency, whether actual or impending military aggression, international treaty verification, or border violation. Joint STARS consists of an airborne platform – an E-8C aircraft with a multi-mode radar system – and US Army mobile Ground Station Modules (GSMs). The E-8C, a modified Boeing 707, carries a phased-array radar antenna in a radome under the forward part of the fuselage. The radar is capable of providing targeting and battle management data to all Joint STARS operators, both in the aircraft and in ground station modules. These operators, in turn, can call on aircraft, missiles or artillery for fire support. JSTARS aircraft have 17 operations consoles and one navigation/self-defence console. A console operator can carry out sector search focusing on smaller sectors and automatically track selected targets. Signal processing techniques are implemented through four high-speed data processors, each capable of performing more than 600 million operations per second.

SPECIFICATIONS

Primary Role:	ground surveillance
Crew:	up to 34
Contractor:	Northrop Grumman
Length:	46.6m (152.9ft)
Wingspan:	44.4 m (145.75ft)
Height:	12.9m (42.5ft)
Maximum Take-off Weight:	152,727kg (336,000lb)
Powerplant:	4 x JT3D-3B turbojets
Thrust:	8182kg (18,000lb) each
Maximum Speed:	945km/h (590mph)
Ceiling:	12,802m (42,000ft)
Range:	unknown
Armament:	none
Systems:	radar, UHF radios, HF radios, VHF radios, SINCGARS, SATCOM, SCDL, JTIDS
Date Deployed:	1996

E-767 AWACS

The Boeing E-767 AWACS (Airborne Warning and Control System) has been selected by the Japanese government to carry out airborne surveillance and command and control operations for tactical and air defence forces. The surveillance system is based on a flexible, multi-mode radar which enables AWACS to separate maritime and airborne targets from ground and sea clutter radar returns. Production of the Boeing 707 airframe ended in May 1991. Following studies of the most suitable follow-on aircraft for the AWACS mission, Boeing announced in December 1991 that it would offer a modified 767 as the platform for the system. The first two aircraft were delivered to the government of Japan in March 1998, and the final two aircraft were delivered in January 1999. All four aircraft entered service with the Japanese Air Self-Defence Force (JASDF) in May 2000. The main AWACS operations cabin behind the flight deck is laid out in equipment bays for communications, data and signal processing, navigation and identification equipment. The AWACS officers and operator stations are equipped with Hazeltine command and control consoles fitted with high-resolution colour displays. The main signal and data processing computer, the CC-2E, has a main storage capacity of over three million words.

SPECIFICATIONS

Primary Role:	AWACS
Crew:	21
Contractor:	Boeing
Length:	48.51m (159.2ft)
Wingspan:	47.57m (156.1ft)
Height:	15.85m (52ft)
Maximum Take-off Weight:	175,000kg (385,000lb)
Powerplant:	2 x General Electric CF6-80C2B6FA turbofans
Thrust:	27,955kg (61,500lb) each
Maximum Speed:	800km/h (500mph)
Ceiling:	12,222m (40,100ft)
Range:	10,370km (6481 miles)
Armament:	none
Systems:	AN/APY-2 radar, Lockheed Martin CC-2E signal and data processing computer
Date Deployed:	2000

EA-6B PROWLER

The EA-6B Prowler is the primary tactical jamming aircraft of the US Navy, US Air Force and the US Marine Corps. The aircraft operates from aircraft carriers and from forward land bases. Its mission is to accompany the strike forces and to carry out armed reconnaissance, electronic warfare and jamming operations. The Prowler is carried on all classes of the US Aircraft Carrier fleet: *Enterprise*, *Nimitz*, *Kitty Hawk*, *John F. Kennedy* and *Forrestal*. Its primary naval role is to protect US or allied carrier groups and aircraft by countering hostile radar and jamming enemy communications. It also carries out electronic surveillance tasks and provides defence against incoming anti-ship missiles. The aircraft is crewed by a pilot and three electronic counter-measures (ECM) officers. The forward section of the cockpit accommodates the pilot on the port side and one ECM officer station equipped with the communications and navigation systems, and the defensive ECM including the decoy dispensers. The rear cockpit accommodates two ECM officers and the ALQ-99 control and display stations. The Prowler carries five ALQ-99 tactical jamming pods, two under each wing and one under the fuselage. Each pod houses two powerful continuous wave (CW) transmitters which use beam steering to direct the jamming signal at the threat.

SPECIFICATIONS

Primary Role:	*electronic warfare*
Crew:	*4*
Contractor:	*Grumman*
Length:	*17.98m (59ft)*
Wingspan:	*16.15m (53ft)*
Height:	*4.57m (15ft)*
Maximum Take-off Weight:	*27,954kg (61,500lb)*
Powerplant:	*2 x Pratt & Whitney J52-P408 turbofans*
Thrust:	*5090kg (11,200lb) each*
Maximum Speed:	*976km/h (610mph)*
Ceiling:	*12,192m (40,000ft)*
Range:	*1563km (977 miles)*
Armament:	*four hardpoints for HARM (High Speed Anti-Radiation Missile)*
Systems:	*ALQ-99F tactical jammer*
Date Deployed:	*1977*

EC-130H COMPASS CALL/RIVET FIRE

Compass Call is the designation for a modified version of Lockheed's C-130 Hercules aircraft configured to perform tactical command, control and communications countermeasures (C3CM). Targeting command and control systems provides commanders with an immense advantage both before and during air operations. Compass Call provides a non-lethal means of denying and disrupting enemy command and control, degrading his combat capability and reducing losses to friendly forces. Modifications to the aircraft include an electronic countermeasures system (Rivet Fire), an air refuelling capability and associated navigation and communications systems. Compass Call is subject to worldwide deployment in support of tactical air/ground forces on very short notice. The Compass Call EC-130H is flown by the 355th Wing's 41st and 43rd Electronic Combat Squadrons. Aided by the automated system, the crew analyze the signal environment, designate targets and ensure the system is operating effectively. In a war situation, a signal may be received and linguists on board the aircraft analyze it to determine if it is an enemy signal. If there is a threat, enemy communications would be jammed. On the back of the aircraft is microwave-powered equipment which sends out high-energy radio frequency or interference.

SPECIFICATIONS

Primary Role:	*control and communications countermeasures*
Crew:	*13*
Contractor:	*Lockheed Martin*
Length:	*29.7m (97.75ft)*
Wingspan:	*40.41m (132.6ft)*
Height:	*11.6m (38.25ft)*
Maximum Take-off Weight:	*79,545 kg (175,000lb)*
Powerplant:	*4 x Allison T56-A-15 turboprops*
Thrust:	*6724kg (14,793lb) each*
Maximum Speed:	*602km/h (376mph)*
Ceiling:	*10,060m (33,005ft)*
Range:	*8793km (5496 miles)*
Armament:	*none*
Systems:	*electronic countermeasures system*
Date Deployed:	*1986*

ES-3A SHADOW

The ES-3A is a high-winged, twin-engine, carrier-based electronic reconnaissance mission aircraft equipped with folding wings, a launch bar and tailhook. The heart of the Shadow is an avionics suite based on the Aries II system of the land-based EP-3E Orion. The Shadow's fuselage is packed with sensor stations and processing equipment, and the exterior sports over 60 antennae. The ES-3A Shadow crew is comprised of two pilots and two systems operators. Advanced sensor, navigation and communications systems allow the Shadow's crew to collect extensive data and distribute high-quality information through a variety of channels to the carrier battle group. This gives the battle group commander a clear picture of potential airborne, surface and sub-surface threats. Missions flown by the detachment include over-the-horizon targeting, strike support and reconnaissance. All 16 ES-3 aircraft are essentially modified S-3 Viking airframes, whose submarine detection and other maritime surveillance equipment was removed and the weapons bay fitted with avionics racks to accommodate the ES-3's sensors. The first ES-3A was delivered in 1991. In 1998, the navy made the decision to retire the Shadow early, due to cost implications. All Shadows are now in storage, but may return to service in the future.

SPECIFICATIONS

Primary Role:	*electronic warfare*
Crew:	*4*
Contractor:	*Lockheed Martin*
Length:	*16.26m (53.3ft)*
Wingspan:	*20.93m (68.6ft)*
Height:	*6.93m (22.75ft)*
Maximum Take-off Weight:	*23,882kg (52,540lb)*
Powerplant:	*2 x General Electric TF34-GE-2 turbofans*
Thrust:	*4516kg (9935lb) each*
Maximum Speed:	*814km/h (508mph)*
Ceiling:	*10,363m (34,000ft)*
Range:	*5560km (3475 miles)*
Armament:	*none*
Systems:	*full-spectrum RF receivers, DF equipment, inverse synthetic aperture radar, FLIR, ESM*
Date Deployed:	*1991*

F-14 TOMCAT

The F-14 Tomcat is the US Navy's carrier-based two-seat air defence, intercept, strike and reconnaissance aircraft. The variable-sweep wings and twin upright tail fins of the F-14 Tomcat give the aircraft its distinctive appearance. The variable-sweep wings are set at 20 degrees for take-off, loitering and landing, and automatically change to a maximum sweep of 68 degrees, which reduces drag for high subsonic to supersonic speeds. The wings are swept at 75 degrees for aircraft carrier stowage. The F-14 is armed with a General Electric Vulcan M61A-1 20mm gun with 675 rounds of ammunition, which is mounted internally in the forward section of the fuselage on the port side. The aircraft has eight hardpoints for carrying ordnance, four on the fuselage and two each side under the fixed section of the wings. The aircraft was developed by Northrop Grumman to replace the F-4 Phantom fighter and entered service with the US Navy in 1972. In 1987 the F-14B with an upgraded engine went into production. Further upgrades to the aircraft's radar, avionics and missile capability resulted in the F-14D Super Tomcat which first flew in 1988. The US Navy currently operates 338 F-14 aircraft of all three variants. The aircraft continues to receive phased improvements and is due to remain in service until 2007.

SPECIFICATIONS

Primary Role:	carrier-based multirole fighter
Crew:	2
Contractor:	Grumman Aerospace
Length:	18.6m (61.75ft)
Wingspan:	19m (64ft) to 11.4m (38ft)
Height:	4.8m (16ft)
Maximum Take-off Weight:	32,805kg (72,900lb)
Powerplant:	2 x F-110-GE-400 turbofans
Thrust:	12,150kg (27,000lb) each
Maximum Speed:	2470km/h (1544mph)
Ceiling:	16,154m (53,000ft)
Range:	2965km (1853 miles)
Armament:	1 x 20mm cannon; 4 x AIM-7 or 4 x AIM-54; 4 x AIM-9 or 2 x AIM-9 and 2 x AIM-7
Systems:	AN/APG-71, TARPS, AN/ALE-39 & 29
Date Deployed:	1972

F-15C EAGLE

The F-15 Eagle is an all-weather, highly manoeuvrable tactical fighter designed to gain and maintain air superiority in air combat. The Eagle's air superiority is achieved through a mixture of manoeuvrability, acceleration, range, weapons and avionics. It has electronic systems and weaponry to detect, acquire, track and attack enemy aircraft while operating in friendly or enemy controlled airspace. Its weapons and flight control systems are designed so one person can safely and effectively perform air-to-air combat. It can penetrate enemy defences, outperform and outfight current or projected enemy aircraft. The F-15's superior manoeuvrability and acceleration are achieved through high engine thrust-to-weight ratio and low-wing loading. Low wing-loading (the ratio of aircraft weight to its wing area) is a vital factor in manoeuvrability and, combined with the high thrust-to-weight ratio, enables the F-15 to turn tightly without losing speed. The F-15C is an improved version of the original F-15A single-seat air superiority fighter. Additions incorporated into the F-15C include upgrades to the avionics as well as increased internal fuel capacity and a higher allowable gross take-off weight. The F-15C has an air combat victory ratio of 95:0, making it one of the most effective air superiority aircraft ever developed.

SPECIFICATIONS

Primary Role:	*tactical fighter*
Crew:	*1*
Contractor:	*McDonnell Douglas*
Length:	*19.43m (63.75ft)*
Wingspan:	*13.05m (42.75ft)*
Height:	*5.63m (18.47ft)*
Maximum Take-off Weight:	*36,741kg (81,000lb)*
Powerplant:	*2 x FlOO-P-220 turbofans*
Thrust:	*10,659kg (23,450lb) each*
Maximum Speed:	*2655km/h (1659mph)*
Ceiling:	*18,290m (60,000ft)*
Range:	*5745km (3590 miles)*
Armament:	*1 x M-61A1 20mm gun, 4 x AIM-9L/M and 4 x AIM-7F/M*
Systems:	*AN/APG-70 radar, IFF, AN/ALQ-135(V), AN/ALQ-128, RWR, AN/AVQ-26, LANTIRN*
Date Deployed:	*1972*

F-15D EAGLE

The F-15D is a two-seat variant of the F-15C. The primary purpose of the F-15D is aircrew training, with an instructor occupying the rear seat while an upgrading pilot mans the front seat. A multi-mission avionics system sets the F-15 apart from other fighter aircraft. It includes a Head-Up Display (HUD), advanced radar, inertial navigation system, flight instruments, UHF communications, tactical navigation system and instrument landing system. It also has an internally mounted tactical electronic-warfare system, identification friend or foe (IFF) system, electronic countermeasures (ECM) set and a central digital computer. The HUD projects on the windscreen all essential flight information gathered by the integrated avionics system. This display, visible in any light conditions, provides the pilot with information necessary to track and destroy an enemy aircraft without having to look down at cockpit instruments. The F-15's radar can look up at high-flying targets and down at low-flying targets without being confused by ground clutter. It can also detect and track aircraft and small, high-speed targets at distances beyond visual range down to close range, and at altitudes down to tree-top level. For close-in dog fights, the radar automatically acquires enemy aircraft, and this information is projected on the HUD.

SPECIFICATIONS

Primary Role:	*tactical fighter*
Crew:	*2*
Contractor:	*McDonnell Douglas*
Length:	*19.43m (63.75ft)*
Wingspan:	*13.05m (42.75ft)*
Height:	*5.63m (18.47ft)*
Maximum Take-off Weight:	*36,741kg (81,000lb)*
Powerplant:	*2 x FlOO-P-220 turbofans*
Thrust:	*10,659kg (23,450lb) each*
Maximum Speed:	*2655km/h (1659mph)*
Ceiling:	*18,290m (60,000ft)*
Range:	*5745km (3590 miles)*
Armament:	*1 x M-61A1 20mm gun, 4 x AIM-9 and 4 x AIM-7*
Systems:	*AN/APG-70 radar, IFF, AN/ALQ-135(V), AN/ALQ-128, RWR, AN/AVQ-26, LANTIRN*
Date Deployed:	*1972*

F-15E STRIKE EAGLE

The F-15E is especially configured for the deep strike mission. The Strike Eagle accomplishes this mission by expanding on the capabilities of the air superiority F-15, adding a rear-seat weapon systems operator (WSO) crew member, and incorporating new avionics. The F-15E performs day and night all-weather air-to-air and air-to-ground missions including strategic strike and interdiction. Although primarily a deep interdiction platform, the F-15E can also perform close air support and escort missions. Strike Eagles are equipped with LANTIRN, enhancing night precision guided munitions (PGM) delivery capability. The F-15E inboard wing stations and the centerline can be loaded with various armaments. The outboard wing hardpoints are unable to carry heavy loads and are assigned for electronic countermeasures (ECM) pods. The other hardpoints can be employed for various loads with the use of multiple ejection racks (MERs). Each MER can hold six Mk 82 bombs or "Snakeye" retarded bombs, or six Mk 20 "Rockeye" dispensers, four CBU-52B, CBU-58B, or CBU-71B dispensers, or a single Mk 84 bomb. The F-15E can also carry "smart" weapons: the CBU-10 laser-guided bomb based on the Mk 84 bomb, CBU-12, CBU-15 and AGM-65 Maverick air-to-ground missiles.

SPECIFICATIONS

Primary Role:	long-range interdiction
Crew:	2
Contractor:	McDonnell Douglas
Length:	19.45m (63.8ft)
Wingspan:	13.05m (42.8ft)
Height:	5.64m (18.5ft)
Maximum Take-off Weight:	36,818kg (81,000lb)
Powerplant:	2 x F100-PW-229 turbofans
Thrust:	13,227kg (29,100lb) each
Maximum Speed:	2655km/h (1650mph)
Ceiling:	20,000m (65,000ft)
Range:	5600km (3500 miles)
Armament:	4 x AIM-9, 4 x AIM-7, AMRAAM); CBU-10, -12, -15 and -24, AGM-65,1 x 20mm
Systems:	Raytheon AN/APG-70 synthetic aperture radar, HUD, LANTIRN
Date Deployed:	1987

F-16C FIGHTING FALCON

The F-16 Fighting Falcon is a multirole fighter. It is highly manoeuvrable and has proven itself in air-to-air combat and air-to-surface attack. In an air combat role, the F-16's manoeuvrability and combat radius exceed that of all potential enemy fighter aircraft. It can locate targets in all-weather conditions and detect low-flying aircraft in radar ground clutter. The F-16 can fly more than 860km (500 miles), deliver its weapons with superior accuracy, defend itself against enemy aircraft, and return to its starting point. In designing the F-16, advanced aerospace science and proven reliable systems from other aircraft such as the F-15 and F-111 were selected. These were combined to simplify the aircraft and reduce its size, maintenance costs and weight. With a full load of internal fuel, the F-16 can withstand up to nine Gs – nine times the force of gravity – which exceeds the capability of other fighter aircraft. The cockpit and its bubble canopy give the pilot unobstructed forward and upward vision, and the seat-back angle was expanded from the usual 13 degrees to 30 degrees, increasing pilot comfort and gravity force tolerance. The pilot has excellent flight control of his F-16 through its "fly-by-wire" system. The F-16C is the current single-seat version of this excellent aircraft.

SPECIFICATIONS

Primary Role:	*multirole fighter*
Crew:	*1*
Contractor:	*Lockheed Martin*
Length:	*14.8m (48.55ft)*
Wingspan:	*9.8m (32.15ft)*
Height:	*4.8m (15.74ft)*
Maximum Take-off Weight:	*16,875kg (37,500lb)*
Powerplant:	*1 x F100-PW-229 turbofan*
Thrust:	*12,150kg (27,000lb)*
Maximum Speed:	*2400km/h (1500mph)*
Ceiling:	*15,000m (50,000ft)*
Range:	*3900km (2437 miles)*
Armament:	*1 x 20mm cannon, AMRAAM, AIM-7, AIM-9, AGM-88 HARM, Harpoon, Penguin*
Systems:	*RWR, Raytheon AN/ALQ-184, TACAN, IFF, FOTD*
Date Deployed:	*1979*

F-16D FIGHTING FALCON

The F-16D is the two-seat trainer version of the aircraft. Avionics systems include a highly accurate inertial navigation system in which a computer provides steering information to the pilot. The aircraft has UHF and VHF radios plus an instrument landing system. It also has a warning system and modular countermeasure pods to be used against airborne or surface electronic threats; the fuselage also has space for additional avionics systems. The Fibre Optic Towed Decoy (FOTD) provides aircraft protection against radar-guided missiles to supplement traditional radar-jamming equipment. The device is towed at varying distances behind the aircraft while transmitting a signal like that of a hostile radar. The missile will detect and lock onto the decoy rather than the aircraft. This is achieved by making the decoy's radiated signal stronger than that of the aircraft. The F-16C and F-16D aircraft, which are the single- and two-seat counterparts to the earlier F-16A and B, incorporate the latest cockpit control and display technology. All F-16s delivered since November 1981 have built-in structural and wiring provisions and systems architecture that permit expansion of the aircraft's multirole flexibility to perform precision strike, night attack and beyond-visual-range interception missions.

SPECIFICATIONS

Primary Role:	multirole fighter
Crew:	2
Contractor:	Lockheed Martin
Length:	14.8m (48.56ft)
Wingspan:	9.8m (32.15ft)
Height:	4.8m (16ft)
Maximum Take-off Weight:	17,045kg (37,500lb)
Powerplant:	1 x F100-PW-229 turbofan
Thrust:	12,150kg (27,000lb)
Maximum Speed:	2400km/h (1500mph)
Ceiling:	15,000m (50,000ft)
Range:	3900km (2437 miles)
Armament:	1 x 20mm cannon, AMRAAM, AIM-7, AIM-9 AAMs, HARM; Harpoon, Penguin
Systems:	AN/ALR-56M, Elta EL/L-8240 ECM, TACAN, FOTD
Date Deployed:	1979

F/A-18 HORNET

The F/A-18 Hornet is a single- and two-seat, twin
engine, multi-mission fighter/attack aircraft that can
operate from either aircraft carriers or land bases. The
F/A-18 fills a variety of roles: air superiority, fighter escort,
suppression of enemy air defences, reconnaissance, forward
air control, close and deep air support, and day and night
strike missions. The F/A-18 has a digital control-by-wire
flight control system which provides excellent handling
qualities, and allows pilots to learn to fly the aircraft with
relative ease. At the same time, this system provides exceptional manoeuvrability and allows the pilot to concentrate
on operating the weapons system. Following a successful run
of more than 400 A and B models, the US Navy began taking
fleet deliveries of improved F/A-18C (single seat) and F/A-
18D (dual seat) models in September 1987. These Hornets
carry the Advanced Medium Range Air-to-Air Missile
(AMRAAM) and the infrared imaging Maverick air-to-
ground (AGM) missile. The multi-mission F/A-18E/F
"Super Hornet" strike fighter is an upgrade of the combat-
proven F/A-18C/D variant. Roll-out of the first Super
Hornet occurred in September 1995, and it flew for the
first time in November 1995. The specifications at right are
for the C/D model.

SPECIFICATIONS

Primary Role:	*multirole attack aircraft*
Crew:	*1*
Contractor:	*McDonnell Douglas*
Length:	*17.07m (56ft)*
Wingspan:	*11.43m (37.5ft)*
Height:	*4.66m (15.28ft)*
Maximum Take-off Weight:	*25,401kg (56,000lb)*
Powerplant:	*2 x F404-GE-400 turbofans*
Thrust:	*14,545kg (32,000lb) each*
Maximum Speed:	*2082km/h (1301mph)*
Ceiling:	*15,240m (50,000ft)*
Range:	*3336km (2085 miles)*
Armament:	*1 x 20mm cannon; AMRAAM, SLAM, Harpoon, AGM-65; AGM-88 HARM*
Systems:	*IDECM, ALE-50 Towed Decoy, ALR-67(V)3 RWR, APG-73 radar*
Date Deployed:	*1983*

F-22 RAPTOR

The F-22 Raptor advanced tactical fighter aircraft is being developed for service with the US Air Force from the year 2005. During flight tests, the F-22 has demonstrated the ability to "supercruise": flying at sustained speeds of over Mach 1.5 without the use of afterburner. The F-22 construction is 39 percent titanium, 24 percent composite, 16 percent aluminum and 1 percent thermoplastic. Titanium is used for its high strength-to-weight ratio in critical stress areas, including some of the bulkheads, and also for its heat-resistant qualities in the hot sections of the aircraft. Carbon-fibre composites have been used for the fuselage frame, doors, intermediate spars on the wings, and for the honeycomb sandwich construction skin panels. The F119-100 low-bypass afterburning turbofan engine is the first fighter aircraft engine equipped with hollow, wide-chord fan blades. The total requirement is estimated to be 339 aircraft. The cockpit is fitted with hands-on throttle and stick (HOTAS) controls. The primary multifunction display provides a view of the air and ground tactical situation, including threat identity, threat priority and tracking information. Two other displays provide communication, navigation, identification and flight information. Three secondary displays show air and ground threat information.

SPECIFICATIONS

Primary Role:	*air superiority fighter*
Crew:	*1*
Contractor:	*Boeing/Lockheed Martin/ General Dynamics*
Length:	*18.90m (62.08ft)*
Wingspan:	*13.56m (44.5ft)*
Height:	*5.08m (16.67ft)*
Maximum Take-off Weight:	*27,216kg (60,000lb)*
Powerplant:	*2 x F119-PW-100 engines*
Thrust:	*15,909kg (35,000lb) each*
Maximum Speed:	*1600km/h (1000mph)*
Ceiling:	*unknown*
Range:	*unknown*
Armament:	*AIM-9 Sidewinders; AMRAAM, 1 x 20mm gun, JDAM*
Systems:	*AN/APG-77, RWR, JTIDS, identification friend or foe (IFF)*
Date Deployed:	*2005 (estimate)*

F-117A NIGHTHAWK

The F-117A Nighthawk is the world's first operational aircraft designed to exploit low-observable stealth technology. The size of an F-15 Eagle, it is powered by two General Electric F404 turbofan engines and has quadruple-redundant fly-by-wire flight controls. Air refuelable, it supports worldwide commitments and adds to the deterrent strength of US military forces. The F-117A can employ a variety of weapons, and is equipped with sophisticated navigation and attack systems integrated into an advanced digital avionics suite that increases mission effectiveness and reduces pilot workload. Detailed planning for missions into highly defended target areas is accomplished by an automated mission planning system developed to take advantage of the unique capabilities of the F-117A. The 49th Fighter Wing serves as the only F-117 Home Station, and provides full flightline maintenance capabilities as well as back-shop support, and the 49th Operations Group operates and maintains the F-117A aircraft. The 8th and 9th Fighter Squadrons are designated to employ the F-117A Nighthawk in combat. The F-117 usually deploys in support of contingency operations, as directed by National Command Authorities. Depending on the deployment duration, varying levels of extra maintenance support may also be deployed.

SPECIFICATIONS

Primary Role:	*fighter/attack*
Crew:	*1*
Contractor:	*Lockheed Martin*
Length:	*20.3m (66.6ft)*
Wingspan:	*13.3m (43.63ft)*
Height:	*3.8m (12.46ft)*
Maximum Take-off Weight:	*23,814kg (52,500lb)*
Powerplant:	*2 x F404-GE turbofans*
Thrust:	*9818kg (21,600lb) each*
Maximum Speed:	*1040km/h (646mph)*
Ceiling:	*unknown*
Range:	*unlimited with refuelling*
Armament:	*Paveway II, Paveway III, BLU 109, WCMD, B61*
Systems:	*FLIR, DLIR, AP-102 mission control, IRADS*
Date Deployed:	*1982*

JOINT STRIKE FIGHTER

The F-35 is the result of the US Defense Department's Joint Strike Fighter (JSF) programme, which sought to build a multirole fighter optimized for the air-to-ground role, designed to meet the needs of the air force, navy, Marine Corps and allies within cost affordability, with improved survivability, precision engagement capability, the mobility necessary for future joint operations, and the reduced life-cycle costs associated with future defence budgets. By using many of the same technologies developed for the F-22, the F-35 will be able to capitalize on commonality and modularity to maximize affordability. Lockheed Martin, the eventual winner of the JSF competition, developed four versions of the Joint Strike Fighter to fulfil the needs of the US armed forces and Great Britain's Royal Air Force and Royal Navy. All versions have the same fuselage and internal weapons bay, plus common outer mold lines with similar structural geometries, identical wing sweeps, and comparable tail shapes. The weapons are stored in two parallel bays located aft or rear of the main landing gear. The canopy, radar, ejection system, subsystems and avionics are all common among the different versions. The same core engine, based on the F119 built by Pratt & Whitney, powers the different versions of the F-35.

SPECIFICATIONS

Primary Role:	*strike fighter*
Crew:	*1*
Contractor:	*Lockheed Martin*
Length:	*13.71m (45ft)*
Wingspan:	*10.97m (36ft)*
Height:	*unknown*
Maximum Take-off Weight:	*22,727kg (50,000lb)*
Powerplant:	*1 x JSF119-611 turbofan*
Thrust:	*15,909kg (35,000lb)*
Maximum Speed:	*unknown*
Ceiling:	*unknown*
Range:	*1120km (700 miles)*
Armament:	*unknown*
Systems:	*AESA radar, ECM, electro-optical targeting system, DAIRS, HUD*
Date Deployed:	*2008*

KC-10A EXTENDER

The KC-10A tanker/cargo aircraft carries out its missions without dependence on overseas bases and without depleting critical fuel supplies in the theatre of operations. Equipped with its own refuelling receptacle, it can support the deployment of fighters, fighter support aircraft and airlifters from US bases to anywhere in the world. The aerial refuelling capability of the KC-10A nearly doubles the non-stop range of a fully loaded C-5 strategic transport. In addition, its cargo capability enables the United States to deploy fighter squadrons and their unit support personnel and equipment with a single aircraft type, instead of requiring both tanker and cargo variants. The US Air Force calls the KC-10A the "Extender" because of its ability to carry out aerial refuelling and cargo mission without forward basing, thus extending the mobility of US forces. To facilitate the handling of cargo, the KC-10A is equipped with a versatile system to accommodate a broad spectrum of loads. The system, adapted in part from the commercial DC-10, has been enhanced with the addition of powered rollers, powered winch provisions for assistance in the fore and aft movement of cargo, an extended ball mat area to permit loading of larger items, and cargo pallet couplers that allow palletizing of cargo items too large for a single pallet.

SPECIFICATIONS

Primary Role:	aerial refuelling/transport
Crew:	4
Contractor:	Douglas Aircraft
Length:	54.4m (178.47)
Wingspan:	50m (164ft)
Height:	17.4m (57ft)
Maximum Take-off Weight:	265,500kg (590,000lb)
Powerplant:	3 x General Electric CF-6-50C2 turbofans
Thrust:	23,625kg (52,500lb) each
Maximum Speed:	990km/h (619mph)
Ceiling:	12,727m (42,000ft)
Range:	7040km (4400 miles)
Armament:	none
Systems:	advanced aerial refuelling boom
Date Deployed:	1981

KC-130

The KC-130 is a multirole tactical tanker/transport which provides the support to US Marine Air Ground Task Forces. It provides inflight refuelling to both tactical aircraft and helicopters as well as rapid ground refuelling when required. Additional tasks performed are aerial delivery of troops and cargo, emergency re-supply into unimproved landing zones within the objective or battle area, airborne Direct Air Support Centre, emergency medevac, tactical insertion of combat troops and equipment, evacuation missions, and support of special operations. The KC-130 is equipped with a removeable 136.26-litre (3600-gallon) steel fuel tank that is carried inside the cargo compartment. The two wing-mounted hose and drogue refuelling pods each transfer up to 1135.5 litres (300 gallons) per minute to two aircraft simultaneously, allowing for rapid cycle times of multiple-receiver aircraft formations (typically four aircraft in less than 30 minutes). Some KC-130s are also equipped with defensive electronic and infrared countermeasures systems. Development is currently under way for the incorporation of night vision lighting, night vision goggle, head-up displays, global positioning system, and jam-resistant radios. The new KC-130J is capable of inflight refuelling of both fixed- and rotary wing aircraft.

SPECIFICATIONS

Primary Role:	*inflight refuelling; tactical transport*
Crew:	*6*
Contractor:	*Lockheed Martin*
Length:	*29.79m (97.75ft)*
Wingspan:	*40.39m (132.6ft)*
Height:	*11.68m (38.3ft)*
Maximum Take-off Weight:	*79,450kg (175,000lb)*
Powerplant:	*4 x T56-A-16 turboprops*
Thrust:	*6724kg (14,793lb) each*
Maximum Speed:	*580km/h (362.25mph)*
Ceiling:	*9140m (30,000ft)*
Range:	*1840km (1150 miles)*
Armament:	*none*
Systems:	*defensive electronic and infrared countermeasures systems*
Date Deployed:	*1962*

KC-135R STRATOTANKER

The KC-135 Stratotanker's primary mission is to refuel long-range bombers. The primary air fuel transfer method is through the tanker's flying boom, controlled by an operator stationed at the rear of the fuselage. A shuttlecock drogue can be trailed behind the boom and used to refuel aircraft equipped with refuelling probes. About 45 US Air Force KC-135R Stratotankers are fitted with Mark 32B wingtip hose and drogue air refuelling pods, which are capable of refuelling US Navy and NATO aircraft which use a probe and drogue system instead of a boom and receptacle. The receiving aircraft approaches the tanker and its probe makes contact with a hose reeled out and trailing from the tanker. The installation of wingtip refuelling pods involves a major modification and refit to the entire aircraft, including modifications to the wing and fuselage fuel tanks, additional fuel-control systems and the installation of indicators and circuit breakers on the flight deck. Inside the refuelling pods, a collapsible funnel-shaped drogue is attached to a hose which is reeled out to trail behind the wing of the aircraft. The hose is fitted with a constant tension spring to give stability to it while it is extended. The F108 turbofans are very fuel efficient, which allows the aircraft to transport more fuel for other aircraft over farther distances.

SPECIFICATIONS

Primary Role:	*aerial refuelling*
Crew:	*4*
Contractor:	*Boeing*
Length:	*40.8m (136.25ft)*
Wingspan:	*39.2m (130.8ft)*
Height:	*11.5m (38.3ft)*
Maximum Take-off Weight:	*146,590kg (322,500lb)*
Powerplant:	*4 x F108-CF-100 turbofans*
Thrust:	*10,000kg (22,224lb) each*
Maximum Speed:	*976km (610mph)*
Ceiling:	*15,152m (50,000ft)*
Range:	*17,907km (11,192 miles)*
Armament:	*none*
Systems:	*FMS-800 integrated flight management system, TCAS, EGPWS, Integrated Processing Centres*
Date Deployed:	*1965*

MC-130E/H COMBAT TALON

The mission of the MC-130E Combat Talon I and MC-130H Combat Talon II is to provide global, day, night and adverse weather capability to airdrop and airland personnel and equipment in support of US Special Forces. The MC-130H conducts infiltrations into politically denied/sensitive defended areas to re-supply or exfiltrate special operations forces and equipment. These aircraft are equipped with inflight refuelling equipment, terrain-following, terrain-avoidance radar, an inertial and global positioning satellite navigation system, and a high-speed aerial delivery system. The special navigation and aerial delivery systems are used to locate small drop zones and deliver people or equipment with greater accuracy and at higher speeds than possible with a standard C-130. Nine of the MC-130Es are equipped with the surface-to-air Fulton air recovery system. It involves use of a large, helium-filled balloon used to raise a nylon lift line. The MC-130E flies towards the lift line at 240km/h (150mph), snags it with scissors-like arms located on the aircraft nose and the person or item of equipment is lifted off, experiencing less shock than that caused by a parachute opening. Aircrew members then use a hydraulic winch to pull the person or equipment aboard the aircraft through the open rear cargo door.

SPECIFICATIONS

Primary Role:	support of special operations
Crew:	4 or 5
Contractor:	Lockheed Martin
Length:	MC-130E, 30.7m (100.8ft); MC-130H, 30.4m (99.75ft)
Wingspan:	40.4m (132.6ft)
Height:	11.7m (38.5ft)
Maximum Take-off Weight:	70,454kg (155,000lb)
Powerplant:	4 x T56-A-15 turboprops
Thrust:	6724kg (14,793lb) each
Maximum Speed:	480km/h (300mph)
Ceiling:	10,000m (33,000ft)
Range:	4976km (3110 miles)
Armament:	none
Systems:	AN/APQ-170 radar, narrow band SATCOM (NBS), DAMA modems, SINCGARS, ACP
Date Deployed:	1966

P-3C ORION

The P-3A was first operational in the United States Navy in 1962. The P-3C version entered service in 1969 and has been continuously upgraded and updated with new avionics systems and mission equipment. The aircraft is flown on missions up to 14 hours long. The flight deck accommodates the pilot, the co-pilot and the flight engineer. The main cabin is configured as a mission operations room for the tactical coordinator, the navigator and communications operator, two operators for the acoustic sensor suite, the electromagnetic sensors systems operator (responsible for the operation of the radar, electronic support measures, infrared detection system and magnetic anomaly detectors), the ordnance crew member and the flight technician. Circular protruding windows in the main cabin give the crew a 180-degree view. The aircraft can carry weapons in the bomb bay and on 10 underwing pylons. The bomb bay is in the underside of the fuselage forward of the wing. US Navy P-3C aircraft are equipped to carry the Harpoon AGM-84 anti-ship and stand-off land attack missile. More than 700 P-3 aircraft have been built by Lockheed Martin. It carries the United States Navy designation P-3, the Canadian Forces designations CP-140 Aurora and the CP-140A Arcturus, and the Spanish designation P-3.

SPECIFICATIONS

Primary Role:	maritime patrol and anti-submarine warfare
Crew:	11
Contractor:	Lockheed Martin
Length:	35.61m (116.8ft)
Wingspan:	30.37m (99.6ft)
Height:	10.27m (33.7ft)
Maximum Take-off Weight:	61,235kg (134,717lb)
Powerplant:	4 x T56-A-14 turboprops
Thrust:	3661kg (8054lb) each
Maximum Speed:	760km/h (475mph)
Ceiling:	8500m (27,887ft)
Range:	3800km (2375 miles)
Armament:	Harpoon, SLAM, AGM 65, MK-46/50 torpedoes, mines
Systems:	AN/APS-137(V), AN/ARR-78(V), ASQ-81, ASA-65, ALQ-78(V)
Date Deployed:	1962

RC-135 RIVET JOINT

The basic airframe of the RC-135 resembles that of the slightly larger Boeing 707 from which it is derived. The interior seats 32 people, including the cockpit crew, electronic warfare officers, intelligence operators and inflight maintenance technicians. The Rivet Joint's modifications are primarily related to its on-board sensor suite, which allows the mission crew to detect, identify and geolocate signals throughout the electromagnetic spectrum. The mission crew can then forward gathered information in a variety of formats to a wide range of consumers via Rivet Joint's extensive communications suite. Having a long service career, RC-135s originally flew from remote bases in Alaska and elsewhere to collect data on Soviet ballistic missile testing during the Cold War. With the use of passive sensors, the RC-135 gathers imagery intelligence (IMINT), telemetry intelligence (TELINT), and signals intelligence (SIGINT). The present RC-135 fleet of 21 aircraft currently consists of four varieties: two RC-135S Cobra Ball, one RC-135X Cobra Eye, two RC-135U Combat Sent, 14 RC-135V/W Rivet Joint, and two RC-135 trainers. The types are assigned to the USAF's 55th Wing, Nebraska. RC-135s saw action during the 1991 Gulf War, supplying intelligence through datalink to AWACS and navy command ships.

SPECIFICATIONS

Primary Role:	*signals intelligence collection*
Crew:	*32*
Contractor:	*Raytheon*
Length:	*41.1m (135ft)*
Wingspan:	*39.9m (131ft)*
Height:	*12.8m (42ft)*
Maximum Take-off Weight:	*133,633kg (297,000lb)*
Powerplant:	*4-x TF33-P-5 turbofans*
Thrust:	*7295kg (16,050lb) each*
Maximum Speed:	*800km/h (500mph)*
Ceiling:	*12,725m (41,750ft)*
Range:	*6500km (4063 miles)*
Armament:	*none*
Systems:	*UHF, VHF, HF, and SATCOM communications, Tactical Digital Information Link, TIBS*
Date Deployed:	*1964*

S-3B VIKING

S-3B aircraft are tasked by carrier battle group commanders to provide anti-submarine warfare and anti-surface warfare, surface surveillance and intelligence collection, electronic warfare, mine warfare, coordinated search and rescue, and fleet support missions, including air wing tanking. The S-3B is a modified S-3A anti-submarine warfare aircraft which has anti-surface warfare capabilities through improvements to various mission avionics and armament systems. It has increased capabilities through improvements to the general-purpose digital computer, acoustic data processor, radar, sonobuoy receiver, sonobuoy reference system, electronic support measures and includes the installation of an electronic countermeasures dispensing system. The S-3B's high-speed computer system processes information generated by the acoustic and non-acoustic target sensor systems. This includes a new inverse synthetic aperture radar. To destroy targets, the Viking employs an impressive array of airborne weaponry. This provides the fleet with a very effective airborne capability to combat the significant threat presented by modern combatants and submarines. Additionally, all S-3B aircraft are capable of carrying an inflight refuelling "buddy" store. This allows the transfer of fuel from the Viking aircraft to other naval aircraft.

SPECIFICATIONS

Primary Role:	anti-submarine/surveillance
Crew:	4
Contractor:	Lockheed Martin
Length:	16.3m (53.3ft)
Wingspan:	20.9m (68.6ft)
Height:	6.9m (22.75ft)
Maximum Take-off Weight:	21,592kg (47,502lb)
Powerplant:	2 x TF-34-GE-400B turbofans
Thrust:	8432kg (18,550lb) each
Maximum Speed:	834km/h (521mph)
Ceiling:	12,192m (40,000ft)
Range:	6085km (3803 miles)
Armament:	AGM-84, AGM-65 , torpedoes, mines, rockets, bombs
Systems:	GPS, MR/RS, UHR/SAR, JTIDS, RTSDL, AN/AYK-23 Digital Computer, EO/IR sensor
Date Deployed:	1975

T-38 TALON

The T-38 Talon is a twin-engine, high-altitude, supersonic jet trainer used in a variety of roles because of its design, economy of operations, ease of maintenance, high performance and exceptional safety record. It is used primarily by the Air Education and Training Command for undergraduate pilot and pilot instructor training. Air Combat Command, Air Mobility Command and the National Aeronautics and Space Administration also use the T-38 in various roles. The T-38 has swept-back wings, a streamlined fuselage and tricycle landing gear with a steerable nose wheel. Two independent hydraulic systems power the ailerons, flaps, rudder and other flight-control surfaces. The instructor and student sit in tandem on rocket-powered ejection seats in a pressurized, air-conditioned cockpit. Critical components are waist high and can thus be easily reached by maintenance crews. Student pilots fly the T-38A to learn supersonic techniques, formations, night and instrument flying and cross-country navigation. More than 60,000 pilots have earned their wings in the T-38A. Test pilots and flight test engineers are trained in the T-38A at the US Air Force Test Pilot School at Edwards Air Force Base. The Air Force Material Command uses T-38As to test experimental equipment such as electrical and weapon systems.

SPECIFICATIONS

Primary Role:	advanced jet pilot trainer
Crew:	2
Contractor:	Northrop Corporation
Length:	14m (46.3ft)
Wingspan:	7.6m (25.25ft)
Height:	3.8m (12.46ft)
Maximum Take-off Weight:	5670kg (12,500lb)
Powerplant:	2 x J85-GE-5 turbojets
Thrust:	1315kg (2900lb) each
Maximum Speed:	1299km/h (812mph)
Ceiling:	16,667m (55,000ft)
Range:	1600km (1000 miles)
Armament:	none
Systems:	GPS, ring-laser gyro-inertial navigation system, collision avoidance system, instrument-flight certified HUD
Date Deployed:	1961

T-45 GOSHAWK

The T-45A Goshawk is the US Navy's two-seat advanced jet trainer. To meet the needs of the US Navy training mission and to ensure aircraft carrier compatibility, several modifications to the basic Hawk airframe were incorporated into the T-45 Goshawk design: new twin nose-wheel with catapult launch T-bar; nosewheel steering for manoeuvring within the confines of the carrier deck; strengthened airframe and undercarriage for catapult launches; relocated speed brakes; provision of under-fuselage tailhook; revised avionics; and modified cockpit layout for compatibility with frontline navy combat aircraft. The cockpit is air-conditioned and pressurized by an engine air-bleed system. The Head-Up Display (HUD) is fitted with a video camera system for post-mission analysis, primary and secondary air data indicators, and weapon-aiming computer and display. The aircraft is not armed but has a single pylon installed under each wing for carrying bomb racks, rocket pods or auxiliary fuel tanks. A single baggage pod can also be carried on the single fuselage centreline pylon. A gunsight supplied by CAI Industries is fitted in the rear cockpit. The US Navy has more than 100 T-45 Goshawks and a total of 234 is planned. The T-45TS pilot training scheme includes advanced simulators and computer-assisted instruction as well as training flight programmes.

SPECIFICATIONS

Primary Role:	*trainer*
Crew:	*2*
Contractor:	*Boeing/BAe*
Length:	*11.97m (39.25ft)*
Wingspan:	*9.38m (30.9ft)*
Height:	*4.27m (14ft)*
Maximum Take-off Weight:	*5909kg (12,758lb)*
Powerplant:	*1 x Adour Mk871 turbofan*
Thrust:	*2604kg (5730lb)*
Maximum Speed:	*1006km/h (625mph)*
Ceiling:	*12,192m (40,000ft)*
Range:	*1532km (958 miles)*
Armament:	*five hardpoints for carriage of training bombs and rockets*
Systems:	*AN/USN-2 AHRS, AN/ARN-144 range and instrument landing system, IFF*
Date Deployed:	*1992*

U-2R

The U-2 is a single-seat, single-engine reconnaissance aircraft which provides continuous day or night, high-altitude, all-weather, stand-off surveillance of an area in direct support of US and allied ground and air forces. Long, wide, straight wings give the U-2 glider-like characteristics. It can carry a variety of sensors and cameras, is an extremely reliable reconnaissance aircraft, and enjoys a high mission completion rate. However, the U-2 can be a difficult aircraft to fly due to its unusual landing characteristics: because of its high-altitude mission, the pilot must wear a full pressure suit. The U-2R, first flown in 1967, is 40 per cent larger than the original U-2 designed by Kelly Johnson in the mid-1950s. Current U-2R models are being re-engined and will be designated as a U-2S/ST. The US Air Force accepted the first U-2S in October 1994. A tactical reconnaissance version, the TR-1A, first flew in August 1981 and was delivered to the air force the next month. Designed for stand-off tactical reconnaissance in Europe, the TR-1 was structurally identical to the U-2R. Operational TR-1As were used by the RAF's 17th Reconnaissance Wing beginning in February 1983. The last U-2 and TR-1 aircraft were delivered to the US Air Force in October 1989. In 1992 all TR-1s and U-2s were redesignated U-2R.

SPECIFICATIONS

Primary Role:	high-altitude reconnaissance
Crew:	1
Contractor:	Lockheed Martin
Length:	19.2m (63ft)
Wingspan:	31.39m (103ft)
Height:	4.8m (16ft)
Maximum Take-off Weight:	18,598kg (41,000lb)
Powerplant:	1 x J75-PW-13B turbojet
Thrust:	7727kg (17,000lb)
Maximum Speed:	800km/h (500mph)
Ceiling:	27,432m (90,000ft)
Range:	6400km (4000 miles)
Armament:	none
Systems:	HR-329 (H-cam) camera, IRIS-III, SENIOR YEAR Defensive System, Airborne Information Transmission System
Date Deployed:	1955

VC-25A – AIR FORCE ONE

The mission of the VC-25A aircraft – Air Force One – is to provide transport for the president of the United States. The presidential air transport fleet consists of two specially configured Boeing 747-200B's – tail numbers 28000 and 29000 – with the designation VC-25A. When the president is aboard either aircraft, or any air force aircraft, the radio call sign is "Air Force One". Principal differences between the VC-25A and the standard Boeing 747, other than the number of passengers carried, are the electronic and communications equipment aboard, its interior configuration and furnishings, self-contained baggage loader, front and aft air stairs, and the capability for inflight refuelling. Accommodation for the president includes an executive suite consisting of a state room (with dressing room, lavatory and shower) and the president's office. A conference/dining room is also available for the president, his family and staff. Other separate accommodations are provided for guests, senior staff, Secret Service and security personnel, and the news media. Two galleys provide up to 100 meals at one sitting. Six passenger lavatories, including disabled access facilities, are provided as well as a rest area and mini-galley for the crew. The VC-25A also has a compartment outfitted with medical equipment and supplies for minor medical emergencies.

SPECIFICATIONS

Primary Role:	*presidential air transport*
Crew:	*26*
Contractor:	*Boeing*
Length:	*70.7m (231.8ft)*
Wingspan:	*59.6m (195.5ft)*
Height:	*19.3m (63.3ft)*
Maximum Take-off Weight:	*378,636kg (833,000lb)*
Powerplant:	*4 x CF6-80C2B1 turbofans*
Thrust:	*25,772kg (56,700lb) each*
Maximum Speed:	*1008km/h (630mph)*
Ceiling:	*13,746m (45,100ft)*
Range:	*12,480km (7800 miles)*
Armament:	*none*
Systems:	*multi-frequency radios for air-to-air, air-to-ground and satellite communications*
Date Deployed:	*1990*

SH-2G SUPER SEASPRITE

The SH-2G Super Seasprites of the Royal Australian Navy (RAN) operate from the ANZAC class frigate, mainly in the primary operational role of surface warfare. Accordingly, the aircraft is equipped with state-of-the-art Forward Looking Infra-Red (FLIR) electronic surveillance and protection equipment, a highly capable multi-mode radar, a cabin-mounted machine gun and the Kongsberg Penguin anti-ship missile. The SH-2G has a crew of two. However, it can also be flown by a single pilot and sensor operator (SENSO), due to the flexible Integrated Tactical Avionics System (ITAS) designed by Kaman and Litton Guidance & Controls. The SH-2G also supports underwater warfare operations by acting as a weapons carrier for other aircraft and ships equipped appropriately to locate and track submarines. The SH-2G is able to detect submarines on or near the surface using its FLIR, radar and Electronic Support Measures (ESM), but is not equipped with acoustic detection equipment. The helicopter can carry a variety of air-deliverable anti-submarine weapons, including lightweight torpedoes and depth charges. Like all RAN helicopters, the SH-2G is capable of many utility operations such as personnel and cargo transport, search and rescue (SAR), and external load-lifting. It can also be used to insert special operations forces covertly.

SPECIFICATIONS

Manufacturer:	Kaman Aerospace
Mission:	ASW, anti-ship
Length:	13.5m (44ft)
Height:	4.6m (15ft)
Rotor Diameter:	13.5m (44ft)
Crew:	2
Propulsion:	2 x GE T700-401
Horsepower:	3300 shaft horsepower
Maximum Speed:	256km/h (159mph)
Cruise Speed:	222km/h (138mph)
Vertical Rate of Climb:	630m/min (2070ft/min)
Range:	1000km (620 miles)
Weight:	3447kg (7600lb)
Date Deployed:	2001
Guns:	cabin-mounted machine gun
Missiles:	Penguin anti-ship missile, torpedo
Systems:	GPS, FLIR, ITAS, ESM

DEFENDER 500

A US-made foreign military sales helicopter, the Defender 500 is a variant of the successful OH-6 series. It is used mainly by the armed forces, being very flexible and offering good all-round capabilities. Its missions differ from that of the OH-6 in that it takes on more roles, including direct air support, anti-tank, reconnaissance, observation and light utility. To this end, the Defender 500 can be equipped with a full complement of weapons systems, and configured either as a Defender Scout or as a Defender TOW (Tube launched, Optical tracked and Wire-guided) anti-tank platform. The Scout variation can be fitted with guns, 70mm Folding Fin Aerial Rockets (FFAR) and a grenade launcher. The TOW version can be fitted with twin TOW pods. To complement its increased firepower, the Defender 500 allows for the mounting of a stabilized, direct-view optical sight in the windshield. Options exist to fit a mast-mounted, multiple field-of-view optical sight, a target tracker, a laser rangefinder, thermal imager, a 16x FLIR for night navigation or targeting, and autopilot. This aircraft is used by 22 countries, ranging from the US through Iraq to El Salvador. It is an effective, flexible and relatively cheap helicopter, capable of delivering good results. However, it is no match for more advanced aircraft that have been developed to excel in specific roles.

SPECIFICATIONS

Manufacturer:	*The Boeing Company*
Mission:	*armed multi-purpose*
Length:	*7.6m (25ft)*
Height:	*2.6m (8ft)*
Rotor Diameter:	*8m (26ft)*
Crew:	*2*
Propulsion:	*1 x Allison T63-A-700*
Horsepower:	*317 shaft horsepower*
Maximum Speed:	*241km/h (149mph)*
Cruise Speed:	*221km/h (137mph)*
Vertical Rate of Climb:	*504m/min (1654ft/min)*
Range:	*485km (301 miles)*
Weight:	*896kg (1975lb)*
Date Deployed:	*1962*
Guns:	*40mm grenade launcher, mini-gun*
Missiles:	*TOW, 70mm FFAR*
Systems:	*GPS, FLIR, thermal imager*

CH-113 LABRADOR

C anada's twin-engined CH-113 Labrador helicopter has long been the workhorse of the country's SAR efforts. Originally brought into service in the early 1960s as the Voyageur, it was intended initially to support the Canadian Army. However, it was soon reconfigured from a tactical role to SAR duties, and its name was changed to Labrador. The helicopter has never been configured for military operations per se, but has seen action alongside the Royal Canadian Navy. It is designed with a watertight hull, making it suitable for marine landings. Standard equipment on this rescue craft includes a rescue hoist, a 3500l (770-gallon) long-range fuel tank and a cargo hook capable of holding a 5000kg (11,000lb) load. In addition to these features, the Labrador carries a full complement of emergency medical equipment. It has been at the forefront of SAR operations for the past 35 years, involved in some of the most demanding rescue attempts ever undertaken. The Labrador was used during Operation Saguenay in Quebec, when 14,000 people were evacuated from their flood-ravaged homes. However, the Canadian Government has decided to replace the ageing Labrador with the Cormorant (an adapted version of the EH-101 Merlin). The first one was delivered in 2002, with plans to have 15 in place by 2003.

SPECIFICATIONS

Manufacturer:	The Boeing Company
Mission:	SAR
Length:	25.4m (84ft)
Height:	5.0m (16ft)
Rotor Diameter:	2 x 15.2m (52ft)
Crew:	5
Propulsion:	2 x GE T-58-8F
Horsepower:	2800 shaft horsepower
Maximum Speed:	275km/h (171mph)
Vertical Rate of Climb:	not available
Cruise Speed:	235km/h (147mph)
Range:	1110km (687 miles)
Weight:	9707kg (21,355lb)
Date Deployed:	1967
Guns:	none
Missiles:	none
Systems:	GPS, rescue hoist

CH-124 SEA KING ASW

The CH-124 Sea King ASW (Anti-Submarine Warfare) is a ship-based helicopter with both day- and night-flight capabilities. It is carried aboard many Canadian Maritime Command destroyers, frigates and replenishment ships. The Sea King ASW carries detection, navigation and weapons systems to support its mandate of searching for, locating and destroying submarines. With its sub-surface acoustic detection equipment and homing torpedoes, it is also a versatile surveillance helicopter. In Canada, Sea Kings have become increasingly responsible for SAR operations and disaster relief. They also assist other government departments in carrying out anti-drugs operations, as well as fisheries and pollution patrols. The aircraft has also been instrumental in peacekeeping operations. For example, during the deployment of forces to Somalia, the CH-124 provided troops with logistics, medical and ammunition support, while also flying overland reconnaissance and convoy missions. It was, in effect, the only link soldiers had with the ships, especially during the initial stages of the deployment. This variation of the Sea King family is still used by the Canadian Royal Navy as its principal ASW helicopter, whereas other modern navies have begun to withdraw the Sea King from ASW roles, using them as utility transports.

SPECIFICATIONS

Manufacturer:	Sikorsky Aircraft
Mission:	ASW
Length:	22.2m (72ft)
Height:	5.1m (16ft)
Rotor Diameter:	18.9m (62ft)
Crew:	4
Propulsion:	2 x GE T-58
Horsepower:	2800 shaft horsepower
Maximum Speed:	267km/h (166mph)
Cruise Speed:	167km/h (104mph)
Vertical Rate of Climb:	435m/min (1435ft/min)
Range:	616km (991 miles)
Weight:	5382kg (11,865lb)
Date Deployed:	1963
Guns:	1 x 7.62mm machine gun
Missiles:	Mk.46 homing torpedoes
Systems:	GPS, MAD

CH-146 GRIFFON

U sed exclusively by the Canadian armed forces, the CH-146 Griffon is a customized version of the popular Bell 412 helicopter. It is used as Canada's Utility Transport Tactical Helicopter (UTTH) and provides a robust, reliable and cost-effective capability. Its duties include airlift of equipment and personnel, command and liaison flights, surveillance and reconnaisance, casualty evacuation, logistic transport, SAR, anti-drugs tasks and domestic relief operations. The Griffon is the workhorse of the Canadian armed forces. It has been involved in conducting humanitarian relief operations at home and abroad, including Operation Saguenay in Quebec during the floods of 1996 and in Honduras in 1998. The aircraft is also used to support annual maintenance on the High Arctic Data Communications System (HADACS) on Ellesmere Island. The CH-146 has seen action in Haiti as part of the United Nations mission, as well as supporting NATO in Kosovo. This helicopter is used primarily for tactical lift and transportation purposes and, as a result, carries no weaponry other than two machine guns for self-defence. However, it can be configured for many different roles including logistic airlift, aero-medical support and casualty evacuation, reconnaissance and surveillance, fire-fighting and communications assistance.

SPECIFICATIONS

Manufacturer:	*Bell Helicopter Textron*
Mission:	*utility tactical*
Length:	*17.1m (56ft)*
Height:	*4.6m (15ft)*
Rotor Diameter:	*14m (46ft)*
Crew:	*3*
Propulsion:	*2 x Pratt & Whitney PT6T-3D*
Horsepower:	*1800 shaft horsepower*
Maximum Speed:	*260km/h (160mph)*
Cruise Speed:	*220km/h (136mph)*
Vertical Rate of Climb:	*409m/min (1350 ft/min)*
Range:	*656km (408 miles)*
Weight:	*3363kg (7400lb)*
Date Deployed:	*1995*
Guns:	*2 x 7.62mm machine guns*
Missiles:	*none*
Systems:	*GPS, FLIR*

CH-149 CORMORANT

A collaborative effort between Britain's Westland Helicopters and Agusta of Italy produced the CH-149 Cormorant. The offspring of these two well-established helicopter manufacturers is one of the most capable aircraft in the world today. Known elsewhere as the Merlin, the aircraft in Canadian service is called the Cormorant. This helicopter has been ordered and delivered to a number of armed forces within the European theatre, including the British Royal Navy. It has also been ordered by Canada as a SAR helicopter, replacing the elderly CH-113 Labrador. The Canadian version is based on the EH-101 Merlin, and saw off other US and European competitors in the Canadian SAR procurement drive. It is capable of operating in the most challenging of conditions, a vital prerequisite for any Canadian helicopter given the harsh climate. The Cormorant has a range and endurance far beyond its Canadian SAR predecessors. It has no military equipment onboard, thanks to its exclusive SAR role, yet it works closely with many other elements of the Canadian armed forces. The CH-149 is an extremely capable aircraft, representing an important addition to the Canadian SAR fleet and becoming a fitting replacement for the long-serving Labrador.

SPECIFICATIONS

Manufacturer:	E H Industries
Mission:	SAR
Length:	22.8m (75ft)
Height:	6.7m (22ft)
Rotor Diameter:	18.6m (61ft)
Crew:	3
Propulsion:	3 x GE T700-T6A1
Horsepower:	6700 shaft horsepower
Maximum Speed:	296km/h (185mph)
Cruise Speed:	275km/h (173mph)
Vertical Rate of Climb:	510m/min (1530ft/min)
Range:	926km (580 miles)
Weight:	7121kg (15,700lb)
Date Deployed:	2002
Guns:	none
Missiles:	none
Systems:	GPS, FLIR, winch

S-70

Unlike many Chinese People's Liberation Army (PLA) aircraft, which are generally inferior copies of Western models, the S-70 is a legitimate original helicopter sold to China by the US during the 1980s. The sale of 24 S-70C Black Hawks to the PLA in 1985 took place during a period of flourishing US/China military relations. This sophisticated aircraft is still used by the PLA, and represents one of China's most prized military assets. As the best helicopter in PLA service, the fast and manoeuvrable S-70C has received much care and attention, along with special enhancements that include the LTN3100VLF weather radar/navigation system and more powerful General Electric T700-701A engines. Remarkably, it is the only helicopter in PLA service that can fly in Tibet's harsh weather conditions. However, due to the deterioration in relations between the US and China, with sanctions in place since 1990, the Black Hawks have been starved of the parts needed to keep them in perfect flying order. It is thought that only a few remain in operating condition. China may be hoping shortly to receive spare parts from the US for these prized aircraft, but details of their condition and current military use are scarce. It is difficult, therefore, to predict the future of the PLA's S-70 Black Hawks.

SPECIFICATIONS

Manufacturer:	Sikorsky Aircraft
Mission:	utility
Length:	19.5m (64ft)
Height:	4.8m (16ft)
Rotor Diameter:	16.5m (53ft)
Crew:	2
Propulsion:	2 x GE T700-701A
Horsepower:	3400 shaft horsepower
Maximum Speed:	296km/h (184mph)
Cruise Speed:	257km/h (160mph)
Vertical Rate of Climb:	472m/min (1550ft/min)
Range:	584km (363 miles)
Weight:	5224 kg (11,516lb)
Date Deployed:	1985
Guns:	2 x 7.62mm machine guns
Missiles:	none
Systems:	LTN3100VLF weather radar

SA 342L GAZELLE

China's PLA obtained eight SA 342L Gazelle anti-tank attack helicopters in the late 1980s. It was part of the Chinese Army's preparation to resist a possible invasion by Soviet armoured troops from the northern border. As the PLA's first generation of attack helicopters, this tiny fleet was used to study and test various anti-tank tactics, giving the PLA invaluable experience of modern anti-armour warfare. The purchase of more units and licensed production were considered, but the end of the Cold War and the restoration of the Sino-Soviet relationship terminated the programme. The Eurocopter/Aerospatiale SA 341/342 Gazelle is a French-built light utility helicopter first flown in 1967. Military missions include attack, anti-tank, anti-helicopter, reconnaissance, utility, transport and training. Like the Chinese S-70, the SA 342L Gazelle has not been copied or reproduced, but still remains in service, often acting as enemy aircraft in exercises. As relations between France and China remain friendly, spare parts and the required maintenance are available. The Gazelle is an exceptionally swift and nimble aircraft which, though lacking the punching-power of heavier or more specialized helicopters, is highly capable. A number of first-rate military powers, including Britain and France, still have the Gazelle in active service.

SPECIFICATIONS

Manufacturer:	Eurocopter
Mission:	anti-tank, ground attack
Length:	11.9m (39ft)
Height:	3.1m (10ft)
Rotor Diameter:	10.5m (34ft)
Crew:	1/2
Propulsion:	1 x Turbomeca IIIB
Horsepower:	600 shaft horsepower
Maximum Speed:	310km/h (193mph)
Cruise Speed:	270km/h (168mph)
Vertical Rate of Climb:	732m/min (2415ft/min)
Range:	735km (459 miles)
Weight:	998kg (2195lb)
Date Deployed:	1987
Guns:	1 x 7.62mm machine gun
Missiles:	HOT, HJ-8 ATM
Systems:	basic flight systems

Z-8

The Z-8 is a Chinese copy of the Eurocopter SA 321 Super Frelon. The licensed manufacturer, Changhe Aircraft Industry Corporation, began the reverse engineering work of the Super Frelon in 1976. The first flight of the Chinese-made version, designated Z-8, took place on 11 December 1985. However, due to a variety of technical problems, only a small number of Z-8s (fewer than 20) have been built 18 years after the first flight. All are operated by the PLA's naval aviation arm. Due to the limitations of its large size, the Z-8 can be stationed only on large replenishment ships or on land airfields. A modified army variant called the Z-8A has been developed but has not yet entered service. Photographs of recent PLA joint exercises showed that some Z-8s were being used to transport and drop marine commandos in the enemy zone, illustrating that they are still an important part of the PLA. While the aircraft has largely been replaced by most first-rate military powers, the Chinese version of the Super Frelon may remain in service for some time. The helicopter can be fitted with a wide range of equipment. For ASW missions, the Z-8 can carry the French-made Thomson Sintra HS-12 dipping sonar. It can also tow a minesweeping countermeasure system for mine clearance, or carry eight 250kg (550lb) mines.

SPECIFICATIONS

Manufacturer:	Changhe Aircraft Industry Corp.
Mission:	ASW
Length:	23m (75ft)
Height:	6.7m (22ft)
Rotor Diameter:	18.9m (62ft)
Crew:	2/3
Propulsion:	3 x WZ-6
Horsepower:	4250 shaft horsepower
Maximum Speed:	315km/h (196mph)
Cruise Speed:	266km/h (166mph)
Vertical Rate of Climb:	300m/min (984ft/min)
Range:	830km (518 miles)
Weight:	3447kg (7600lb)
Date Deployed:	1985
Guns:	none
Missiles:	Yu-7 torpedo
Systems:	dipping sonar, minesweeping gear

Z-9W/G

China's Z-9W/G is the first indigenous anti-tank attack helicopter derived from the license-built Eurocopter AS 565N Panther. Its main armaments are four HJ-8 wire-guided anti-tank guided missiles (ATGMs) with a range of 600–3000m (1968–9842ft). The Z-9G is a modified formal production version derived from the Z-9W. In addition to the four HJ-8 ATGMs, the Z-9G can also carry two 57mm rocket launchers or two 12.7mm machine gun pods. The HJ-8 ATGM is guided by a roof-mounted optical sight for searching and tracking. At the Zhuhai Airshow in 2000, China revealed its TY-90 short-range air-to-air missile (AAM), which is designed specifically for helicopter air combat. This missile could eventually be fitted to the Z-9G. Unlike previous Chinese attempts to copy Western designs, the Z-9 is a genuine effort to license-build the country's own aircraft. To a large extent, China has succeeded with this helicopter. However, there is a question mark over the country's ability to provide the necessary spares and ongoing engineering expertise. Considerable effort has gone into the development of this anti-tank helicopter, but only time will tell if it is successful. It isn't certain that China faces any threat requiring anti-armour capability, but the PLA is still attempting to modernize its aviation armoury.

SPECIFICATIONS

Manufacturer:	*Harbin Aircraft Manufacturing*
Mission:	*anti-tank*
Length:	*13.5m (44ft)*
Height:	*3.5m (12ft)*
Rotor Diameter:	*14m (46ft)*
Crew:	*1/2*
Propulsion:	*2 x Turbomeca Arriel 1C2*
Horsepower:	*1400 shaft horsepower*
Maximum Speed:	*305km/h (190mph)*
Cruise Speed:	*255km/h (159mph)*
Vertical Rate of Climb:	*420m/min (1400ft/min)*
Range:	*1000km (625 miles)*
Weight:	*2050kg (4510lb)*
Date Deployed:	*1995*
Guns:	*2 x 12.7mm machine guns*
Missiles:	*HJ-8 ATGM, 57mm rockets, AAM*
Systems:	*roof-mounted optical sight*

Z-11

The Z-11 is a Chinese copy of the French AS-350B Ecurcuil light helicopter, which was developed in the early 1970s. The programme was officially approved in 1989, and development began in 1992. The first flight of the Z-11 took place in December 1994. It is designed for training, scout, liaison and rescue missions, as well as various civil tasks. Although described by the manufacturer as multi-mission, the future of the helicopter is uncertain due to its limited take-off weight, insufficient armament, low survivability and outdated technology. So far the PLA has ordered only a few (no more than 20) Z-11s for pilot training. The quality of the Chinese copies of Western aircraft often lack genuine airworthiness, and China has generally failed in its attempts to produce an indigenous helicopter capable of meaningful military operations. However, the tactic of buying a few foreign helicopters to copy lives on, despite the obvious drawbacks. The Ecureuil helicopter, as manufactured by Eurocopter, is a popular aircraft the world over, in service with myriad defence agencies. This is testimony to the utility of the design, but the Chinese imitation perhaps lacks the finesse and quality of the original, thereby reducing the military value of the helicopter. The PLA's apparent lack of enthusiasm is leaving the aircraft on the sidelines.

SPECIFICATIONS

Manufacturer:	*Changhe Aircraft Industry Corp.*
Mission:	*light support*
Length:	*13m (43ft)*
Height:	*3.1m (10ft)*
Rotor Diameter:	*13m (43ft)*
Crew:	*2*
Propulsion:	*1 x WZ-8D*
Horsepower:	*not available*
Maximum Speed:	*278km/h (173mph)*
Cruise Speed:	*230km/h (143mph)*
Vertical Rate of Climb:	*474m/min (1555ft/min)*
Range:	*560km (350 miles)*
Weight:	*1120kg (2464lb)*
Date Deployed:	*1994*
Guns:	*none*
Missiles:	*none*
Systems:	*basic flight systems*

A109 HIRUNDO

igh power provided by the A109 Military's twin engines makes it a robust and versatile aircraft. It is a lightweight, eight-seat, multi-purpose helicopter, manufactured by Italy's Agusta. The power available allows mission continuation even in the event of one engine failure. This, together with systems duplication and separation, gives the A109 the survivability necessary for military operations. The integrated 1553 military standard digital data bus-compatible mission equipment package, with the wide range of armament and day/night Target Acquisition & Designation Sight (TADS), makes the A109 a real multi-role light helicopter able to satisfy most military requirements. This versatility allows the aircraft to fill different roles such as anti-tank, scout, light attack, escort, area suppression, patrol and reconnaissance missions, plus transport of men and materials. The A109 is powered by two Pratt & Whitney PW-206C or two Turbomeca Arrius 2K1 turboshaft engines, both with a Full Authority Digital Eletronic Control (FADEC) system. These are mounted side by side and drive a combining gearbox. The A109 is currently in service with the Italian armed forces, as well as in Greece, Argentina, Venezuela and with the British special forces. It is well suited to competing in the cut-throat military procurement arena, given its inherent flexibility and all-round performance.

SPECIFICATIONS

Manufacturer:	Agusta
Mission:	multi-role
Length:	13m (43ft)
Height:	3.3m (10ft)
Rotor Diameter:	11m (36ft)
Crew:	1/2
Propulsion:	2 x Turbomeca Arrius 2K1
Horsepower:	800 shaft horsepower
Maximum Speed:	305km/h (190mph)
Cruise Speed:	265km/h (165mph)
Vertical Rate of Climb:	not available
Range:	565km (353 miles)
Weight:	1415kg (3113lb)
Date Deployed:	1974
Guns:	2 x 7.62mm machine guns
Missiles:	HOT, TOW, FFAR rockets
Systems:	GPS, FLIR, FADEC

A129 MANGUSTA

The Italian Army's A129 Mangusta (Mongoose), armed with anti-tank and area-suppression weapons systems, is intended primarily as an attack helicopter to be used against armoured targets. The aircraft can operate during day, night and all-weather conditions. The A129 Mangusta claims to be a proven hot-climate operator, as demonstrated during its peacekeeping operations – it was employed successfully in Somalia where it proved highly reliable and extremely flexible. When Agusta of Italy developed the Mongoose, it became the first attack helicopter to be designed and produced wholly in Europe. Italy is the only country with this helicopter in its inventory. An escort/scout version of the Mangusta is under development for deployment with airmobile units. The aircraft would also be armed for air-to-air combat. The A129 International, developed from the Mangusta, meets the requirements of today's armed forces for a multi-role combat helicopter that combines high performance and survivability with low support costs. Though it lacks the firepower and technological capabilities of peers such as the AH-1 Cobra or the AH-64D Apache Longbow, it is nonetheless a capable aircraft which can be bought at a much lower cost than its US counterparts.

SPECIFICATIONS

Manufacturer:	*Agusta*
Mission:	*light attack*
Length:	*14.3m (47ft)*
Height:	*3.4m (11ft)*
Rotor Diameter:	*11.9m (39ft)*
Crew:	*2*
Propulsion:	*2 x Piaggio Gem 2 Mk1004D*
Horsepower:	*1500 shaft horsepower*
Maximum Speed:	*313km/h (196mph)*
Cruise Speed:	*240km/h (150mph)*
Vertical Rate of Climb:	*612m/min (979ft/min)*
Range:	*700km (437 miles)*
Weight:	*2520kg (5575lb)*
Date Deployed:	*2001*
Guns:	*2 x 20mm machine guns*
Missiles:	*HOT, TOW, Stinger, rockets*
Systems:	*GPS, FLIR*

AH-7 LYNX

Westland's legendary Lynx is one of the most successful light anti-shipping/submarine helicopters ever built, and has been exported to many countries. The British Army, along with the armed forces of many other nations, has adapted the Lynx design to an anti-tank role, armed in this instance with TOW missiles. Due to its cutting-edge technology semi-rigid titanium rotor-head, the aircraft is superbly manoeuvrable and fast. A stripped-down Lynx still holds the world record for the highest speed achieved by a helicopter. The aircraft is adaptable to a wide variety of missions, contributing to its worldwide popularity. Originally, 113 Lynx AH Mk 1s were supplied to Britain's Army Air Corps as a multi-role helicopter. However, during the Cold War its primary job was as an anti-tank aircraft, given its ability to carry eight TOW anti-tank missiles plus a further eight in the cabin as a reload – a vast improvement over the AH-1 Scout it replaced. The latest Lynx in UK Army Air Corps service is the AH Mk 9, designed as a Light Battlefield Helicopter (LBH). It is an integral part of the hard-hitting new 16th Air Assault Brigade. Despite the Lynx's advanced age, it is likely to remain in service for several more years, although the newer Merlin and Apache helicopters can be expected to take over some of its roles.

SPECIFICATIONS

Manufacturer:	*Westland Helicopters*
Mission:	*anti-tank*
Length:	*12m (39ft)*
Height:	*3.4m (11ft)*
Rotor Diameter:	*12.8m (42ft)*
Crew:	*2*
Propulsion:	*2 x Rolls-Royce Gem 41*
Horsepower:	*1800 shaft horsepower*
Maximum Speed:	*330km/h (206mph)*
Cruise Speed:	*232km/h (145mph)*
Vertical Rate of Climb:	*604m/min (1994ft/min)*
Range:	*528km (330 miles)*
Weight:	*3291kg (7240lb)*
Date Deployed:	*1962*
Guns:	*2 x 7.62mm machine guns*
Missiles:	*TOW*
Systems:	*GPS*

AS 355N ECUREUIL

Eurocopter has found the manufacture of the Ecureuil to be something of a cash cow. It is in service with armed forces, police forces, rescue units and civilian flight schools the world over. More than 3000 of these very adaptable helicopters have been sold internationally. Five UK police forces have already adopted the AS 355N for their operations, but Britain does not operate the Ecureuil in a military role. The major attraction of the AS 355N is the high power provided by its twin Turbomeca Arrius 1A turboshafts, which develop maximum take-off power of 579 shaft horsepower. The low vibration level also helps to reduce noise, a major consideration in urban night-time flying. The spacious cabin of the Ecureuil allows mission-specific equipment to be integrated while retaining excellent visibility. Many of these aircraft in service with law enforcement agencies carry a thermal imaging camera, FLIR and a TV camera package mounted under the machine's nose. They may also have a Nightsun searchlight capable of illuminating a large area from a signficant altitude. The Ecureuil does see military service in France, where it is used as a light utility aircraft in reconnaissance missions, or for command-and-control purposes. Normally without weapons, it can be armed with a machine gun for self-defence if required.

SPECIFICATIONS

Manufacturer:	Eurocopter
Mission:	lightweight utility
Length:	10.9 m (36ft)
Height:	3.1 m (10ft)
Rotor Diameter:	10.7m (35ft)
Crew:	1/2
Propulsion:	2 x Turbomeca Arrius 1A
Horsepower:	579 shaft horsepower
Maximum Speed:	224km/h (140mph)
Cruise Speed:	200km/h (125mph)
Vertical Rate of Climb:	390m/min (1287ft/min)
Range:	700km (440 miles)
Weight:	1305kg (2871lb)
Date Deployed:	1985
Guns:	None
Missiles:	None
Systems:	GPS, FLIR, searchlight

AS 532 COUGAR

The AS 532 Cougar Mk II U2 A2 helicopter has the biggest cabin volume in its category, capable of transporting 29 commandos or 12 stretchers with medical equipment. In addition, it is capable of carrying 5000kg (11,000lb) under-slung on the hook. This version is tasked primarily with combat SAR missions, retrieving downed pilots or special forces teams from deep behind enemy lines, or evacuating injured troops in dangerous battle zones. There is also an armed version, which can be equipped with a 20mm cannon or two pintle-mounted .50in machine guns. Its basic design, with screens in the cockpit and a four-axis autopilot with built-in coupler, makes it possible to reduce the crew workload and increase its safety for tactical flight by the same degree. This highly effective aircraft is primarily in service with the French armed forces, but has also been ordered by Saudi Arabia. For very long-range missions, the combat SAR helicopter can carry auxiliary fuel tanks on the cargo hook. With additional tanks stored internally, the aircraft can travel up to 1120km (700 miles) and back, rescuing two people in the process. For extra endurance and even longer operational range, an in-flight refuelling capability is being developed by the manufacturer in order to boost the helicopter's already impressive performance.

SPECIFICATIONS

Manufacturer:	Eurocopter
Mission:	combat SAR
Length:	16.3m (54ft)
Height:	4.6m (15ft)
Rotor Diameter:	15.6m (51ft)
Crew:	2/3
Propulsion:	2 x Turbomeca Makila 1A2
Horsepower:	3800 shaft horsepower
Maximum Speed:	325km/h (203mph)
Cruise Speed:	262km/h (163mph)
Vertical Rate of Climb:	420m/min (1386ft/min)
Range:	842km (526 miles)
Weight:	4700kg (10,340lb)
Date Deployed:	1996
Guns:	20mm cannon
Missiles:	2.75in rockets
Systems:	GPS, FLIR

AS 532 COUGAR UL

Eurocopter's AS 532 Cougar UL is a multi-mission, twin-engined helicopter which is part of the Horizon radar surveillance system. This technology was developed to counter any possible threat posed by the tank fleets of the Warsaw Pact countries. The system includes a Cougar helicopter with radar and electronic countermeasures (ECM), plus a ground station. The first flight of the Horizon Cougar with the full radar system took place in late 1992, and the French Army took an initial delivery in July 1996. It is also in service with the Swiss Air Force, which ordered 27 aircraft. Another buyer of the Cougar UL is the Turkish Army. The helicopter is equipped with a long-range, multi-mode retractable pulse Doppler radar. A rotating antenna is carried beneath the fuselage, and the radar range is 200km (124 miles). The radar scans a ground area of 20,000km² (12,400 square miles) in 10 seconds, and the data is transmitted to a ground station. The information is then disseminated to relevant parties as a real-time snapshot of the situation on the ground. The Horizon-equipped Cougar reflects the new emphasis being placed on Command, Control, Communications and Intelligence (C3I) and the developing role of heliborne surveillance radar. The aircraft may be unarmed, but it is still an effective force multiplier.

SPECIFICATIONS

Manufacturer:	Eurocopter
Mission:	heliborne surveillance
Length:	16.3m (54ft)
Height:	4.6m (15ft)
Rotor Diameter:	15.6m (51ft)
Crew:	2/3
Propulsion:	2 x Turbomeca Makila 1A1
Horsepower:	3550 shaft horsepower
Maximum Speed:	325km/h (203mph)
Cruise Speed:	262km/h (163mph)
Vertical Rate of Climb:	420m/min (1386ft/min)
Range:	842km (526 miles)
Weight:	4700kg (10,340lb)
Date Deployed:	1996
Guns:	none
Missiles:	none
Systems:	GPS, Horizon radar system

AS 555 FENNEC

The AS 555 Fennec armed lightweight helicopter is a further development of the Aerospatiale AS 350, which flew for the first time in 1976. The Fennec is built by Eurocopter in France, and is used only by Denmark and Singapore. The AS 555 is normally configured for an anti-tank role but can be reconfigured into an unarmed version. It is equipped for instrument flying and can therefore operate in most weather conditions. The crew comprises a pilot and a gunner, who are both protected by armoured seats. In the anti-tank role, the Fennec is equipped with the weapons system HeliTOW. It consists of two TOW launchers with room for two TOW missiles each, an optical sight with 3x or 12x enlargement, a number of computers for calculations, and a control panel placed in front of the gunner. The maximum TOW range is 3.75km (2.4 miles). The Fennec is characterized by the ability to deploy fast and change targets quickly. It can also deploy in a night reconnaissance role as the crew are equipped with Pilots' Night Vision Goggles (PNVG). A major disadvantage of the Fennec is its ineffectiveness against stationary, camouflaged or dug-in targets because they cannot be recognized at long distances by the optical sight – and the helicopter lacks any other method of long-range detection.

SPECIFICATIONS

Manufacturer:	*Eurocopter*
Mission:	*anti-tank*
Length:	*12.9m (42ft)*
Height:	*3.2m (11ft)*
Rotor Diameter:	*10.7m (35ft)*
Crew:	*1/2*
Propulsion:	*2 x Turbomeca Arrius 319-1*
Horsepower:	*520 shaft horsepower*
Maximum Speed:	*278km/h (173mph)*
Cruise Speed:	*217km/h (136mph)*
Vertical Rate of Climb:	*not available*
Range:	*666km (420 miles)*
Weight:	*1382kg (3040lb)*
Date Deployed:	*1993*
Guns:	*machine guns, 20mm cannon*
Missiles:	*TOW, rockets*
Systems:	*GPS, optical sight, PNVG*

AS 565 PANTHER

The AS 565 Panther is the military version of the popular Dauphin helicopter as used by the US Coast Guard. It is capable of transporting up to 10 fully armed commandos into combat zones, performing casualty evacuation and providing logisitical support. The AS 565 SB is the armed version of the shipborne Panther. It can be carried on board a combat vessel such as a destroyer or frigate to improve the vessel's observation, reconnaissance and attack capabilities – augmenting the ship's original detection systems. This Eurocopter-built aircraft can carry a wide variety of weapons, including the MISTRAL and HOT missiles, as well as 70mm FFAR rockets. With a four-blade main rotor, two turboshaft engines are mounted side-by-side on top of the cabin. The teardrop-shaped body features a tapered boom to the tail fin, a rounded nose and stepped-up cockpit. The Panther has a retractable undercarriage and flat underside. The helicopter's tail flats have swept-back tips, mounted forward of the tapered fin. The rotor is inside a housing at the bottom of the fin. A weapons-carrying platform is installed on some models. The Panther is deployed aboard the French Navy Cassard Class anti-air frigates. It is also in service with other countries, carrying out regular operations for the Israeli Defence Force among others.

SPECIFICATIONS

Manufacturer:	*Eurocopter*
Mission:	*light multi-pupose*
Length:	*11.6m (38ft)*
Height:	*3.9m (13ft)*
Rotor Diameter:	*11.9m (39ft)*
Crew:	*2/3*
Propulsion:	*2 x Turbomeca Arriel IMI*
Horsepower:	*1600 shaft horsepower*
Maximum Speed:	*296km/h (184mph)*
Cruise Speed:	*275km/h (171mph)*
Vertical Rate of Climb:	*420m/min (1400ft/min)*
Range:	*875km (547 miles)*
Weight:	*2255kg (4970lb)*
Date Deployed:	*1989*
Guns:	*20mm cannon*
Missiles:	*MISTRAL, HOT, 70mm FFAR*
Systems:	*GPS, FLIR. ORB-32 radar*

EC 635

Eurocopter's EC 635 Light Utility Helicopter (LUH) is the military version of its EC 135 and features the same technology. The EC 635 is a modern, lightweight, twin-engined, eight-seat, multi-role helicopter that makes extensive use of composite materials and crash-resistant seats and fuel system. New-generation, high-set main rotor and shrouded tail rotor systems (Fenestron-type) provide low noise and safe operation. High operational efficiency, adverse weather day/night operations, high performance with power reserve and an advanced maintenance concept are among the key features of the EC 635. Utilizing the aircraft's multi-role capability, the EC 635 is suitable for military and paramilitary operations including utility, training, troop transport, reconnaissance and SAR. Helicopters such as the EC 635, with their exceptional efficiency and great flexibility, have become firm favourites with governments seeking to minimize military expenditure while maintaining effective armed forces. Helicopters in this class promise more capability for less money. Though seldom able to compete with specialized aircraft that have been tailor-made for particular missions, the EC 635 can operate in varied roles with great efficiency. Deployed in 1999, it is due to enter widespread active service over the next few years.

SPECIFICATIONS

Manufacturer:	*Eurocopter*
Mission:	*light utility*
Length:	*10.2m (33ft)*
Height:	*3.5m (11ft)*
Rotor Diameter:	*10.2m (33ft)*
Crew:	*1/2*
Propulsion:	*2 x Turbomeca Arrius 2B1*
Horsepower:	*711 shaft horsepower*
Maximum Speed:	*259km/h (161mph)*
Cruise Speed:	*235km/h (146mph)*
Vertical Rate of Climb:	*456m/min (1500ft/min)*
Range:	*675km (422 miles)*
Weight:	*1490kg (3284lb)*
Date Deployed:	*1999*
Guns:	*20mm cannon*
Missiles:	*70mm FFAR*
Systems:	*GPS*

EC 725 COUGAR

The EC 725 medium-sized, twin-engine helicopter is the latest member of the Cougar family developed by Eurocopter. The French Air Force has a requirement for 14 EC 725s for the combat SAR role, and is scheduled to introduce three into service during 2003. This brand-new aircraft is suitable for a wide range of missions, ranging from tactical troop transport, special operations, SAR, combat SAR and maritime surveillance to humanitarian support, logistic ground support, medical evacuation and shipborne operations. The ferry flight range of the EC 725 Cougar is more than 1500km (925 miles). In the tactical troop transport role, the aircraft can carry 19 soldiers. In the combat SAR role, the EC 725 is able to rescue a downed aircrew at a radius of action of 400km (250 miles). The maximum seat capacity is two crew and 29 troops. The Advanced Helicopter Cockpit and Avionics System (AHCAS) includes an automatic flight control system developed by SAGEM, integrating the flight, navigation and tactical mission data. The helicopter is equipped with radar and FLIR for day- and night-time SAR capability. The navigation suite includes Doppler radar, GPS and inertial navigation system. The helicopter has an extensive weapons-carrying capability, and can be armed with a variety of machine guns and rockets.

SPECIFICATIONS

Manufacturer:	*Eurocopter*
Mission:	*multi-mission*
Length:	*16.3m (54ft)*
Height:	*4.6m (15ft)*
Rotor Diameter:	*16.2m (53ft)*
Crew:	*2*
Propulsion:	*2 x Turbomeca Makila*
Horsepower:	*3800 shaft horsepower*
Maximum Speed:	*325km/h (203mph)*
Cruise Speed:	*262km/h (163mph)*
Vertical Rate of Climb:	*420m/min (1386ft/min)*
Range:	*1480km (920 miles)*
Weight:	*4700kg (10,340lb)*
Date Deployed:	*2003*
Guns:	*2 x 7.65mm machine guns*
Missiles:	*2.75in rockets*
Systems:	*GPS, FLIR, PNVG, AHCAS*

EH 101 MERLIN

Agusta of Italy and Britain's Westland Helicopters, through a venture named EH Industries, collaborated in the design of the highly effective EH 101 Merlin. The joint effort resulted in one of the world's most capable rotary-wing aircraft. Its primary roles consist of ASW, utility transport and SAR. This variation of the Merlin will be replacing the ageing Sea King ASW used by Britain's Royal Navy for its on-board anti-submarine operations. To achieve its mission goals, the Merlin is equipped with some of the most sophisticated systems known to aviation. These include the Blue Kestrel 360-degree radar, allowing the Merlin to operate completely independently in the search for and destruction of targets. It requires no support from other aerial or surface platforms to deliver good results. The Merlin is exceptionally versatile, able to adapt its configuration rapidly to the changing environment and mission goals. Not only is the aircaft versatile in its operational capability, but it is also flexible in the areas it can cover. It is an all-weather, 24-hour-capable helicopter, able to withstand extremes of temperature of plus or minus 50º. The Merlin is recognized as an exceptional machine, and is expected to see service with many nations, and earn Westland much money from foreign export sales.

SPECIFICATIONS

Manufacturer:	EH Industries
Mission:	ASW
Length:	22.8m (75ft)
Height:	6.7m (22ft)
Rotor Diameter:	18.6m (61ft)
Crew:	3
Propulsion:	3 x Rolls-Royce/Turbomeca RTM
Horsepower:	6700 shaft horsepower
Maximum Speed:	296km/h (185mph)
Cruise Speed:	275km/h (173mph)
Vertical Rate of Climb:	510m/min (1530ft/min)
Range:	926km (580 miles)
Weight:	7121kg (15,700lb)
Date Deployed:	1998
Guns:	2 x 7.62mm machine guns
Missiles:	Sea Skua, lightweight torpedoes
Systems:	GPS, FLIR, Blue Kestrel 360º radar

HC-4 SEA KING

Britain's Royal Marines make good use of the HC-4 Sea King Commando. Introduced in the late 1970s, it has seen service wherever the Royal Marines have been in action. It is based on the basic Sea King design, but has additional capabilities and features that differ from the ASW and Airborne Early Warning (AEW) Sea Kings. These include the ability to transport up to 2730kg (6000lb) of equipment slung under the aircraft (including the 105mm Light Gun), to carry 27 fully equipped troops, and to fly in all types of weather. The all-weather capability is an especially useful characteristic since Royal Marines frequently operate in the most hostile environments. In addition, the Sea King Commando can be armed with a 7.62mm General Purpose Machine Gun (GPMG). By some helicopter standards, the Commando has not been in service for a particularly long time. However, the Sea King design is ageing fast, and this highly successful aircraft is to be replaced by the more advanced EH-101 Merlin helicopter. This process has already begun, and will eventually equip the Royal Marines with an even more formidable aircraft. The Sea King Commando saw action during the 1991 Gulf War, where it served with distinction in a most demanding environment.

SPECIFICATIONS

Manufacturer:	Westland Helicopters
Mission:	utility transport
Length:	22.1m (73ft)
Height:	5.1m (17ft)
Rotor Diameter:	18.9m (61ft)
Crew:	3
Propulsion:	2 x Rolls-Royce Gnome H-1400
Horsepower:	3000 shaft horsepower
Maximum Speed:	256km/h (160mph)
Cruise Speed:	208km/h (130mph)
Vertical Rate of Climb:	670m/min (2200ft/min)
Range:	1230km (764 miles)
Weight:	6202kg (13,672lb)
Date Deployed:	1979
Guns:	1 x 7.62mm machine gun
Missiles:	none
Systems:	GPS, basic flight systems

NH-90

The NH-90 began life in the early 1980s under a European multinational development programme for a new multi-purpose transport and naval helicopter, intended to replace the elderly UH-1 Huey, Puma and Sea King aircraft. The NH-90 is designed for survivability, reliability and ease of maintenance. It can be fitted with a FLIR turret in the nose, as well as with defensive countermeasure aids. The NH-90 is available in two forms, the NATO Frigate Helicopter (NFH) and the Tactical Transport Helicopter (TTH). The NFH is intended for ASW and maritime surface warfare, though it can be used for SAR and transport roles. It has an automatic rotor and tail-folding system, plus a combat avionics suite, including a 360-degree search radar in a drum under the fuselage, magnetic anomaly detector (MAD) and dipping sonar or sonobuoys. The TTH variant lacks the offensive avionics systems of the NFH, though it is fitted with weather radar. It has infrared exhaust suppressors; armoured crew seats; a cable cutter; a PNVG-compatible cockpit; plus an optional rear-loading ramp. Standard crew is pilot and copilot, with a payload capacity of 20 troops, 12 stretchers and a light tactical vehicle or 2500kg (5500lb) of cargo. The TTH can be equipped with defensive armament such as chaff and flares, or even with an infrared jammer.

SPECIFICATIONS

Manufacturer:	Eurocopter
Mission:	multi-role transport
Length:	16.1m (53ft)
Height:	5.4m (18ft)
Rotor Diameter:	16.3m (53ft)
Crew:	2
Propulsion:	2 x Rolls-Royce/Turbomeca
Horsepower:	3084 shaft horsepower
Maximum Speed:	300km/h (186mph)
Cruise Speed:	259km/h (160mph)
Vertical Rate of Climb:	480m/min (1584ft/min)
Range:	1204km (650 miles)
Weight:	6428kg (14,741lb)
Date Deployed:	2003
Guns:	none
Missiles:	MU-90 torpedo, Exocet missile
Systems:	sonobuoy, FLIR, MAD

PAH-1

Also known as the BO 105, the PAH-1 is a lightweight, twin-engine, multi-role military helicopter built by Eurocopter. The military version includes the anti-tank variant, with weapon-carrying outriggers; as well as the scout version, which has a mast-mounted sight above the main rotor. Missions include direct air support, anti-tank, reconnaissance, SAR and transportation. In addition to reconnaissance, observation and surveillance missions, this helicopter is particularly suitable for carrying taskforces and casualties, thanks to its unpartitioned cabin/cargo area. The aircraft can be reconfigured with ease for different armed duties. The machine can support the following specific weapon systems: anti-tank missiles; rocket launchers; pod-mounted gun; gun turret; and side-firing machine gun. It has been in service since the early 1970s, and has seen action with more than 40 national armed forces in countries as diverse as Bahrain, Canada and Mexico. The Maritime Search & Surveillance (MSS) BO 105 CBS 5 is the shipborne version. This helicopter features a 360-degree surveillance and meteorological radar. It can also support an associated data recorder and transmitter system, a Doppler/GPS navigation control system, and is PNVG compatible. It can also carry lightweight torpedoes.

SPECIFICATIONS

Manufacturer:	*Eurocopter*
Mission:	*anti-tank, utility*
Length:	*8.8m (29ft)*
Height:	*3.0m (10ft)*
Rotor Diameter:	*9.8m (32 ft)*
Crew:	*2*
Propulsion:	*2 x Allison 250-C20B*
Horsepower:	*3300 shaft horsepower*
Maximum Speed:	*242km/h (151mph)*
Cruise Speed:	*205km/h (128mph)*
Vertical Rate of Climb:	*450m/min (1485ft/min)*
Range:	*555km (345 miles)*
Weight:	*1913kg (4208lb)*
Date Deployed:	*1973*
Guns:	*1 x RH 202 20mm cannon*
Missiles:	*anti-tank missiles, rocket pods*
Systems:	*GPS, weather radar, autopilot*

PAH-2 TIGER

The PAH-2 Tiger owes its existence to a German and French agreement to collaborate on the development of a new advanced-attack helicopter for their armed forces. Ultimately, they settled on two basic versions: an anti-tank model for both countries; and an escort/fire support model for France. The design of the Tiger is typical of contemporary attack helicopters. The slim fuselage seats two crew in a tandem, stepped cockpit. While the German model follows the general trend of placing the gunner in the front seat and the pilot aft, the French prefer the opposite seating arrangement. The Tiger makes extensive use of composite materials both for weight reduction and to improve survivability. Armament is carried on two stub wings, and the French escort model is equipped with a cannon turret under the nose. The French HAC and German UHT models are primarily anti-tank versions equipped with a mast-mounted site and armed with HOT-2 or Trigat missiles. The French HAP, on the other hand, is optimized for air defence and fire support. It is generally armed with a nose cannon turret and air-to-air missiles. The first Tigers were delivered in 2001, and will shortly become fully operational. The helicopter became more recognizable after it had a taste of stardom, featuring in the James Bond movie *Goldeneye*.

SPECIFICATIONS

Manufacturer:	*Eurocopter*
Mission:	*attack*
Length:	*14m (46ft)*
Height:	*4.3m (14ft)*
Rotor Diameter:	*13m (43ft)*
Crew:	*2*
Propulsion:	*2 x Turbomeca/Rolls-Royce MTR*
Horsepower:	*2570 shaft horsepower*
Maximum Speed:	*320km/h (200mph)*
Cruise Speed:	*230km/h (145mph)*
Vertical Rate of Climb:	*640m/min (2105ft/min)*
Range:	*725km (453 miles)*
Weight:	*3300kg (7275lb)*
Date Deployed:	*2001*
Guns:	*1 x GIAT 30mm cannon*
Missiles:	*Stinger, Mistral, Trigat, HOT, FFAR*
Systems:	*GPS, FLIR*

SA 319 ALOUETTE III

No longer in service with most leading military powers, the Eurocopter-built SA 319 Alouette III multi-purpose and light-attack helicopter is a larger and very successful development of the earlier SE 313B Alouette II. In contrast to its predecessor, it has an improved structure, a stronger propulsion system, better equipment and a closed fuselage with cantilevers. The cabin is more spacious and can transport a larger payload. The military version is employed partly for its highly sensitive weapon and radar mechanisms. In an anti-shipping role, the SA 319B is equipped with ORB-31 radar and four AS.11/AS.12 missiles. For the purpose of ASW, the equipment available is the same radar, but with Crouzet MAD and two Mk 46 torpedos. The Alouette III has been phased out by the majority of first-rate military powers, and has been replaced by more modern helicopters. However, in its day the Alouette III was a cutting-edge aircraft. More than 1500 examples were sold in a production run lasting 20 years. A few of these aircraft are still used by less advanced or wealthy armed forces, and they continue to perform well. Romania and Switzerland, as well as India (which calls its licence-built version "Chetak"), still operate the Alouette III, though not generally in the light-attack role for which it was originally designed.

SPECIFICATIONS

Manufacturer:	*Eurocopter*
Mission:	*multi-purpose, light-attack*
Length:	*12.8m (42ft)*
Height:	*3m (10ft)*
Rotor Diameter:	*11m (33ft)*
Crew:	*1*
Propulsion:	*1 x Turbomeca Astazou XIV*
Horsepower:	*700 shaft horsepower*
Maximum Speed:	*220km/h (137mph)*
Cruise Speed:	*190km/h (118mph)*
Vertical Rate of Climb:	*258m/min (851ft/min)*
Range:	*600km (375 miles)*
Weight:	*1108kg (2437lb)*
Date Deployed:	*1973*
Guns:	*1 x 7.62mm machine gun*
Missiles:	*none*
Systems:	*basic flight systems*

SA 321 SUPER FRELON

The Super Frelon first flew in 1962 and began active service in 1966. This record-breaking helicopter was produced as a civilian transport version and in military transport, ASW and anti-ship guise. The Super Frelon is powered by three Turbomeca Turmo IIIC turbo-shafts married to a Fiat-built transmission system and Sikorsky-designed rotor head and blades. The six-blade main rotor is mounted above-centre of the fuselage. Of the three engines, two are mounted side-by-side atop the fuselage forward of the main rotor; the third is behind the main rotor. It has a boat hull-type fuselage that mounts stabilizing floats on either side of the body, which has fixed landing gear and an upswept rear section. The Super Frelon owes its existence to a French Ministry of Defence requirement for a large military troop transport helicopter, and was produced in both troop transport and ASW configurations. The successful aircraft was sold to a number of countries including Israel, South Africa and Libya. This powerful helicopter has broken several records, including the world speed record in 1963 at 341km/h (211mph) over 3km (2 miles) – unfortunately, now surpassed. The French Navy is beginning to phase out the Super Frelon, replacing it with the much more modern and capable Eurocopter-built NH-90 by 2005.

SPECIFICATIONS

Manufacturer:	Eurocopter
Mission:	assault transport
Length:	23m (75ft)
Height:	6.7m (22ft)
Rotor Diameter:	18.9m (62ft)
Crew:	5
Propulsion:	3 x Turbomeca Turmo IIIC
Horsepower:	3150 shaft horsepower
Maximum Speed:	270km/h (168mph)
Cruise Speed:	248km/h (155mph)
Vertical Rate of Climb:	300m/min (984ft/min)
Range:	700km (437 miles)
Weight:	6863kg (15,098lb)
Date Deployed:	1966
Guns:	2 x 7.62mm machine guns
Missiles:	none
Systems:	GPS, IFF, PNVG

SA 330 PUMA

Britain's Royal Air Force (RAF) first deployed the SA 330 Puma in 1971. This familiar helicopter was designed as a tactical transport vehicle; and various other versions, including the Super Puma, are now in service worldwide. Selection of the design arose from an RAF requirement to replace obsolete Belvedere and Whirlwind helicopters then in service. The Puma can operate as a casualty evacuation aircraft, transport for up to 16 fully equipped troops, and as a medium-lift transport carrying up to 2500kg (5500lb) of freight using under-fuselage hardpoints to sling loads externally. The Puma can also function effectively as a helicopter gunship capable of carrying a wide variety of armament. The aircraft is capable of being airlifted in a number of transport aircraft types with the minimum of work. Like the Chinook, the Puma is equipped with night vision aids, defensive ECM systems and advanced navigation aids. It is operated by many countries in various guises and configurations, although Britain and France are looking for a replacement for their ageing Puma fleets. The Puma has seen extensive operational use, including in the 1991 Gulf War, in the Balkans conflict and in counter-terrorist operations in Northern Ireland. It has been an asset to Britain's helicopter forces for three decades.

SPECIFICATIONS

Manufacturer:	*Westland Helicopters*
Mission:	*utility*
Length:	*15.5m (51ft)*
Height:	*4.92m (16ft)*
Rotor Diameter:	*15m (50ft)*
Crew:	*2*
Propulsion:	*2 x Turbomeca Makila*
Horsepower:	*3500 shaft horsepower*
Maximum Speed:	*278km/h (173mph)*
Cruise Speed:	*249km/h (155mph)*
Vertical Rate of Climb:	*420m/min (1386ft/min)*
Range:	*850km (531 miles)*
Weight:	*4370kg (9614lb)*
Date Deployed:	*1971*
Guns:	*1 x 7.62mm machine gun*
Missiles:	*none*
Systems:	*GPS, PNVG*

SA 341 GAZELLE

The Gazelle is another example of European collaboration in helicopter design and development. Designed primarily by Aerospatiale, the predecessor to the Eurocopter group, the British version was built under licence by Westland. The Gazelle is used by the British Army Air Corps, primarily as a scout helicopter, and designated the AH Mk1. It is small, light, exceptionally nimble and quick and is thus ideally suited to this role. It began life as an anti-tank helicopter, armed with missiles and rockets, although it has largely been replaced by more capable aircraft. The Gazelle was therefore re-designated as an observation and reconnaissance helicopter. It has seen action in almost every military confrontation in which British forces have been involved in since it came into service. It played a valuable amphibious role in the Falklands conflict, performed well in the deserts of Kuwait and Iraq, as well as operating effectively during the more recent Kosovo campaign. Indeed, it continues to serve in the reconnaissance role with the British Army, and can be expected to do so for some time. In the French Army, it is employed in a very similar scouting role to that in the UK. France, too, has found more modern and capable anti-tank helicopters, but still sees tangible battlefield value in the size, speed and agility of the Gazelle.

SPECIFICATIONS

Manufacturer:	*Westland Helicopters*
Mission:	*reconnaissance*
Length:	*11.9m (39ft)*
Height:	*3.1m (10ft)*
Rotor Diameter:	*10.5m (34ft)*
Crew:	*1/2*
Propulsion:	*1 x Turbomeca Astazou XIVM*
Horsepower:	*600 shaft horsepower*
Maximum Speed:	*310km/h (193mph)*
Cruise Speed:	*270km/h (168mph)*
Vertical Rate of Climb:	*732m/min (2415ft/min)*
Range:	*670km (418 miles)*
Weight:	*998kg (2195lb)*
Date Deployed:	*1973*
Guns:	*1 x 7.62mm machine gun*
Missiles:	*HOT, 2.75in rockets*
Systems:	*PNVG, laser sight*

WAH-64D APACHE

More than 60 WAH-64D Apache Longbow helicopters are being procured for the British Army. The aircraft is based on the Boeing AH-64D Apache Longbow which entered service with the US Army in 1998. The formidable surveillance and target acquisition capability of the sensor suite, together with other improvements in weapon systems and avionics, means that the Westland Apache will represent a significant increase in capability when compared with the Lynx Mk.7 TOW currently in service with the British Army. It will be a fully digitized platform which, when linked to other weapon systems, will be capable of revolutionizing the battlefield of the future. The Westland Apache presents a completely new capability, with implications for the British Army's organization, training, logistics and peace-time infrastructure. The Westland-built British Army version of the Apache has some special characteristics. The RTM322 engines offer significant improvement in performance, while the radio has been upgraded to the new digital BOWMAN system due to enter the British armed forces. Another UK-specific feature is HIDAS (Helicopter Integrated Defensive Aids System), developed by Marconi and providing an integrated suite of radar, laser and missile-warning sensors and countermeasures.

SPECIFICATIONS

Manufacturer:	*Westland Helicopters*
Mission:	*attack*
Length:	*15.5m (51ft)*
Height:	*5m (16ft)*
Rotor Diameter:	*14.6m (48ft)*
Crew:	*2*
Propulsion:	*2 x RTM322*
Horsepower:	*3000 shaft horsepower*
Maximum Speed:	*360km/h (225mph)*
Cruise Speed:	*261km/h (163mph)*
Vertical Rate of Climb:	*737m/min (2432ft/min)*
Range:	*410km (256 miles)*
Weight:	*5352kg (11,774lb)*
Date Deployed:	*2001*
Guns:	*1 x M230 30mm chain gun*
Missiles:	*Hellfire, CRV-7, Stinger, Sidewinder*
Systems:	*FLIR, TADS, HIDAS, Longbow radar*

WASP HAS 1

The Wasp was based on the British Army Scout helicopter and was originally named Sea Scout. Many trials were carried out with prototype aircraft to assess the viability of operating small helicopters in an anti-submarine role from frigates. When these trials were shown to be a success, greatly increasing such a ship's ASW capability, Britain's Royal Navy ordered the Wasp HAS 1. The first production model was delivered in 1963, and a total of 98 Wasp HAS 1s were ultimately built for the Royal Navy. The type served on Royal Navy frigates until the late 1970s when it was replaced by the Lynx. However, the Wasp had an unexpected reprieve in 1982 when several old frigates, incapable of operating the Lynx, were re-commissioned due to the Falklands conflict. Indeed, a Wasp helicopter aboard the Royal Navy frigate HMS *Plymouth* crippled the Argentine submarine *Santa Fe* in South Georgia at the start of the war, by firing an AS-12 missile through the submarine's conning tower. After this campaign, the Wasp was withdrawn from service when the last of the older frigates was decommissioned in 1988. While the Wasp is generally being replaced by more modern and capable aircraft, it still serves in many air forces and navies around the world, including those of Malaysia and New Zealand, although in ever-decreasing numbers.

SPECIFICATIONS

Manufacturer:	*Westland Helicopters*
Mission:	*light reconnaissance*
Length:	*12.9m (40ft)*
Height:	*2.7m (9ft)*
Rotor Diameter:	*9.8m (32ft)*
Crew:	*1/2*
Propulsion:	*1 x Rolls-Royce Bristol Nimbus 503*
Horsepower:	*710 shaft horsepower*
Maximum Speed:	*193km/h (120mph)*
Cruise Speed:	*179km/h (111mph)*
Vertical Rate of Climb:	*not available*
Range:	*670km (418 miles)*
Weight:	*1566kg (3452lb)*
Date Deployed:	*1963*
Guns:	*1 x 7.62mm machine gun*
Missiles:	*rockets, torpedoes*
Systems:	*basic flight systems*

WESSEX

The Wessex is the old lady of the British armed forces' helicopter fleet. It first flew in 1966 and continues in service to this day, though in a much reduced capacity. Originally used as a light support helicopter, Westland's Wessex was initially capable of carrying 12 fully equipped troops or 3500kg (7700lb) of underslung cargo, including light artillery pieces and vehicles. Based on the successful Sikorsky S-58 design, the Wessex has two different engines to increase its capabilities. The venerable aircraft has served with Britain's RAF for more than 30 years. Those aircraft still active are the last of around 60 ordered for the RAF, and are used as light support helicopters (and SAR units in Cyprus) capable of carrying an increased load of 16 fully equipped troops. Previous RAF roles included SAR, training and transport duties with The Queen's Flight. The Wessex also saw extensive action in the Falklands conflict, where it took part in a number of special forces actions with the Special Air Service (SAS) and Special Boat Service (SBS). In its SAR role, much of its time was spent in search of civilians who had become stranded at sea or lost on mountains. Although it was on 24-hour standby to rescue downed pilots, it excelled in rescuing civilians and undoubtedly saved hundreds of lives over the course of its operational life.

SPECIFICATIONS

Manufacturer:	*Westland Helicopters*
Mission:	*SAR and support*
Length:	*14.7m (48ft)*
Height:	*4.9m (16ft)*
Rotor Diameter:	*17m (66ft)*
Crew:	*2*
Propulsion:	*2 x Rolls-Royce Gnome 112/113*
Horsepower:	*1600 shaft horsepower*
Maximum Speed:	*212km/h (132mph)*
Cruise Speed:	*195km/h (121mph)*
Vertical Rate of Climb:	*480m/min (1584ft/min)*
Range:	*630km (390 miles)*
Weight:	*3455kg (7600lb)*
Date Deployed:	*1966*
Guns:	*none*
Missiles:	*none*
Systems:	*not available*

HAL DHRUV

Designed and developed by Hindustan Aeronautics Ltd (HAL), the Dhruv Advanced Light Helicopter (ALH) is a modern, efficient and highly cost-effective multi-role helicopter. It is an indigenously designed and developed aircraft, something of a rarity outside the US and Europe. The Dhruv was conceived to meet the requirements of the Indian Army, Navy, Air Force and the Coastguard. It has been designed with great flexibility in mind and, as such, it can be configured as an armed gunship, a utility transport, an ASW/anti-ship helicopter and a platform for SAR and casualty evacuation. The Dhruv, deployed in 2002, is powered by two Turbomeca TM-333 turbo-shaft engines procured from France. These units are being produced under licence in India by HAL. Large rear clamshell doors allow easy loading of stretchers or other bulky loads. It is simple to fly and economical to maintain. From its inception, the Dhruv has been designed in close cooperation with the military, bringing their expertise and requirements into the design process. With sonar/sonics, radar, ESM, torpedoes, depth charges and anti-ship missiles, the Dhruv can be an effective ASW or anti-shipping aircraft. Similarly, with the turret gun, rockets, air-to-air missiles and third-generation anti-tank missiles, it is also a useful battlefield asset.

SPECIFICATIONS

Manufacturer:	*Hindustan Aeronautics Ltd*
Mission:	*light multi-role*
Length:	*12.9m (43ft)*
Height:	*3.4m (11ft)*
Rotor Diameter:	*13.2m (44ft)*
Crew:	*2*
Propulsion:	*2 x Turbomeca TM-333-2B*
Horsepower:	*1800 shaft horsepower*
Maximum Speed:	*280km/h (175mph)*
Cruise Speed:	*245km/h (153mph)*
Vertical Rate of Climb:	*540m/min (1782ft/min)*
Range:	*800km (500 miles)*
Weight:	*2505kg (5511lb)*
Date Deployed:	*2002*
Guns:	*2 x 20mm machine guns*
Missiles:	*ATGM, AAM, rockets, torpedoes*
Systems:	*GPS*

MI-6 HOOK

When it was unveiled to the world in 1957, the Mil Mi-6 had no rival as the world's biggest helicopter. Designed as a large transport for military and commercial applications, the Mil Mi-6 stunned Western observers with its sheer size. NATO gave the giant helicopter the codename Hook. However, the Mi-6 is capable of carrying loads in other ways than merely using a hook. A two-winged rear door swings open to accommodate bulky loads. Additional cargoes can be attached externally. Extra fuel tanks are another option for attachment to two stubby wings extending sideways just aft of the rotor shaft, offering additional fuel capacity. The Mi-6 was produced mainly by the Kazan aircraft factory from 1968 until about 1980. As well as the Indian armed forces, buyers have been found in Belarus, Bulgaria, Egypt, Iraq, Poland, Peru and Vietnam. As spare parts for the huge transport aircraft have become expensive, the Mi-6 has been pushed out of the heavy-duty airlifting market by the newer and still larger Russian-built Mil Mi-26 Halo. A few Hooks can still be seen in Siberia, although many seem no longer to be airworthy. However, the Indian Air Force has kept a few of these ageing aircraft in service, though they have been largely replaced by the more modern Halo, which appears to be cheaper to maintain.

SPECIFICATIONS

Manufacturer:	*Mil/Kazan*
Mission:	*heavy transport*
Length:	*33m (109ft)*
Height:	*9.7m (32ft)*
Rotor Diameter:	*35m (115ft)*
Crew:	*5*
Propulsion:	*2 x Soloviev D-25V*
Horsepower:	*10,850 shaft horsepower*
Maximum Speed:	*300km/h (186mph)*
Cruise Speed:	*250km/h (156 miles)*
Vertical Rate of Climb:	*not available*
Range:	*1000km (625 miles)*
Weight:	*27,240kg (60,054lb)*
Date Deployed:	*1959*
Guns:	*none*
Missiles:	*none*
Systems:	*internal auto-loading system*

MI-25 HIND D

An export version of the standard Russian Mi-24 Hind D helicopter, India's Mi-25 Hind D isn't as modern as the Mi-35 export version of the Mi-24 Hind E. That said, there are very few differences between these individual aircraft, save varying avionics and doctrine. As with a great many nations around the world, the Indian armed forces have been attracted by the awesome firepower of the Hind series of helicopters, as well as by their ability to transport troops into combat. The Mi-25 is exceptionally well armed. It has a nose-mounted, four-barrelled 12.7mm gatling gun with 1400 rounds of ammunition and a high rate of fire. In addition, it can carry up to 4200kg (9240lb) of ordnance, which could include the UV-57-32 57mm unguided rocket pods, ATGMs, AAMs or even iron "dumb" bombs on six wing pylons. Internally, the Mi-25 can carry up to eight fully armed troops or four stretchers for casualty evacuation. India's Mi-25s have seen action along the Kashmiri border region in suppressing rebel activity, and are on constant standby in the event of war with neighbouring Pakistan. The Indian Hinds also saw action in the war against the Tamil Tigers in Sri Lanka. The missiles that the Mi-25 carries are capable of knocking out enemy armour at a range of more than 8km (5 miles), while the 57mm rockets can destroy soft targets at ranges in excess of 4km (2.5 miles).

SPECIFICATIONS

Manufacturer:	*Mil Helicopter Factory*
Mission:	*attack, transport*
Length:	*18.5m (61ft)*
Height:	*6.5m (21ft)*
Rotor Diameter:	*17.3m (57ft)*
Crew:	*2*
Propulsion:	*2 x Isotov TV3-117*
Horsepower:	*4450 shaft horsepower*
Maximum Speed:	*335km/h (210mph)*
Cruise Speed:	*295km/h (185mph)*
Vertical Rate of Climb:	*750m/min (2460ft/min)*
Range:	*450km (281 miles)*
Weight:	*8500kg (18,700lb)*
Date Deployed:	*1976*
Guns:	*1 x 12.7mm chain gun*
Missiles:	*AT-6, 57mm rockets, AA-8 Aphid*
Systems:	*FLIR, RWR, laser-designator*

MI-35 HIND E

The Mi-35 is the most recent export variation of the Russian-built Mi-24 Hind E. It is essentially the same highly effective aircraft, although there are some minor differences. The Mi-35 is armed with anti-tank missile systems for the engagement of moving armoured targets, weapon emplacements and slow-moving air targets. The aircraft retains its useful troop transport capability. The Mi-35 been exported to many countries including Angola, Bulgaria, Cuba, India, Iraq and North Korea. The two crew (pilot and weapons operator) are accommodated in tandem armoured cockpits with individual canopies and flat, bulletproof glass windscreens. The main cabin can accommodate eight fully equipped troops or four stretchers. The Mi-35 is fitted with a YakB four-barrelled, 12.7mm, built-in, flexibly mounted machine gun, which has a firing rate of 4000–4500 rounds per minute and a muzzle velocity of 860mps (2821fps). It is also armed with the Shturm ATGM system. Shturm (NATO designation AT-6 Spiral) is a short-range missile with semi-automatic radio command guidance. The 5.4kg (12lb) high-explosive fragmentation warhead is capable of penetrating up to 650mm (26in) of armour. Iraq is believed still to have some of these very capable Mi-35 attack and transport helicopters, but apparently hides them carefully.

SPECIFICATIONS

Manufacturer:	Mil Helicopter Factory
Mission:	attack, transport
Length:	18.5m (61ft)
Height:	6.5m (21ft)
Rotor Diameter:	17.3m (57ft)
Crew:	2
Propulsion:	2 x Isotov TV-3117
Horsepower:	4450 shaft horsepower
Maximum Speed:	335km/h (210mph)
Cruise Speed:	295km/h (185mph)
Vertical Rate of Climb:	750m/min (2460ft/min)
Range:	450km (281 miles)
Weight:	8500kg (18,700lb)
Date Deployed:	1976
Guns:	1 x 12.7mm chain gun
Missiles:	AT-6 Shturm, 57mm rockets
Systems:	FLIR, RWR, laser designator

PETEN

As operated by the IAF, the AH-64A Peten is an older version of the renowned US-built Apache attack helicopter. The Longbow radar-equipped AH-64D is now being brought into Israeli service, but the most common version is the AH-64A. The firepower and capability of the Peten (meaning adder in Hebrew) is both well-known and feared. US-operated Apaches were highly effective during the 1991 Gulf War. The Apache entered Israeli service earlier than expected in 1990, after the original customer, ironically Kuwait, was invaded by Iraq. The design and avionics are identical to the US versions, with a few tweaks to adapt the aircraft to the Middle Eastern environment. Like the Israeli Tzefa, the Peten has seen a great deal of action in its first 12 years of service. It has been used in counter-terrorist operations against Palestinian and Lebanese guerrillas, scoring some remarkable successes in taking down senior terrorist leaders. Petens are fitted with 30mm automatic cannon, FFAR rockets and the fearsome Hellfire air-to-ground missile. The Longbow radar capability of the AH-64D version is somewhat redundant in the urban environments of the Palestinian territories, which makes the continued use of the less complex and technologically advanced AH-64A a sensible and cost-effective decision.

SPECIFICATIONS

Manufacturer:	*The Boeing Company*
Mission:	*multi-mission attack*
Length:	*17.7m (58ft)*
Height:	*4m (13ft)*
Rotor Diameter:	*14.6m (48ft)*
Crew:	*2*
Propulsion:	*2 x GE T700-701C*
Horsepower:	*1940 shaft horsepower*
Maximum Speed:	*365km/h (227mph)*
Cruise Speed:	*265km/h (165mph)*
Vertical Rate of Climb:	*450m/min (1475ft/min)*
Range:	*407km (253 miles)*
Weight:	*7800kg (17,000lb)*
Date Deployed:	*1990*
Guns:	*1 x 30mm automatic cannon*
Missiles:	*FFAR, Hellfire AGM*
Systems:	*TADS, PNVG, HADSS*

SAIFAN

The first two IAF Jet Rangers arrived in Israel in June 1971, and the type was nicknamed Saifan. Besides their regular role as light transports and VIP helicopters, the Saifans were also employed for casualty evacuation and pursuit of enemy forces. Other roles include directing Israeli ground fire against enemy positions and general reconnaissance. These helicopters have seen much of the action during Israel's recent conflicts, including the Yom Kippur War and the Palestinian *Intifada*. The Saifans also saw a great deal of action during the 1991 Gulf War. In an effort to drag Israel into the war, and thus destabilize the Allied coalition, Iraq launched Scud missiles at cities throughout Israel. There was widespread fear that these could contain chemical or biological agents capable of killing thousands of civilians. Every time Iraqi Scud missiles were launched against Israel, Saifans were scrambled to locate the point of impact, to determine whether the missile contained a chemical warhead and to direct SAR forces to the spot. The Saifan uses the same Bell 206 airframe as the US OH-58D Kiowa Warrior, and the Jet Ranger design is one of the most successful helicopters ever designed. It is in service in more than 30 countries around the world, in many guises.

SPECIFICATIONS

Manufacturer:	*Bell Helicopter Textron*
Mission:	*light multi-purpose*
Length:	*9.5m (31ft)*
Height:	*2.9m (10ft)*
Rotor Diameter:	*10.2m (34ft)*
Crew:	*2*
Propulsion:	*1 x Allison 250-C20J*
Horsepower:	*420 shaft horsepower*
Maximum Speed:	*225km/h (140mph)*
Cruise Speed:	*216km/h (135mph)*
Vertical Rate of Climb:	*384m/min (1267ft/min)*
Range:	*748km (467 miles)*
Weight:	*742kg (1632lb)*
Date Deployed:	*1971*
Guns:	*none*
Missiles:	*none*
Systems:	*GPS, NBC agent detectors*

TZEFA

srael began a heavy defence procurement programme after the Yom Kippur War of October 1973, when the Israeli Defence Force (IDF) had initially failed to halt the Syrian armoured assault on the Golan Heights and the Egyptian crossing of the Suez Canal. Dense Arab air defences proved a deadly hindrance to Israeli Air Force (IAF) operations. Attack helicopters were seen as the solution, and this need provided the IAF with an incentive to procure attack helicopters of its own. The Cobra, or Tzefa as it is known in Hebrew, was selected to fulfil the Israeli procurement request and has been in service with the IDF since 1975. Given Israel's turbulent recent history, the Tzefa has probably seen more action than any other aircraft in Israeli service. It has been used in every theatre and at every level of conflict in which the IDF has been involved, including counter-terrorist operations against *Hizbullah*, as well as full-scale war in Lebanon. The first Tzefa attack took place on 9 May 1979, against a terrorist structure located inside a refugee camp near Tyre. The deadly aircraft continues to attack targets within Israeli and Palestinian territories. The use of Tzefa gunships in urban areas has been criticized in some sections of the international press but, in terrain where ground troops are easy targets for snipers, the helicopter is particularly effective.

SPECIFICATIONS

Manufacturer:	*Bell Helicopter Textron*
Mission:	*fire-support, attack*
Length:	*13.8m (45ft)*
Height:	*4.4m (14ft)*
Rotor Diameter:	*14.6m (48ft)*
Crew:	*2*
Propulsion:	*1 x Lycoming T53-L-703*
Horsepower:	*1800 shaft horsepower*
Maximum Speed:	*290km/h (181mph)*
Cruise Speed:	*227km/h (141mph)*
Vertical Rate of Climb:	*494m/min (1630ft/min)*
Range:	*507km (316 miles)*
Weight:	*2939kg (6465lb)*
Date Deployed:	*1975*
Guns:	*1 x M197 20mm turreted cannon*
Missiles:	*TOW, 40mm grenade gun*
Systems:	*GPS, FLIR*

YANSHUF

In 1997, Israel ordered its first newly built Black Hawks, or Yanshufs as they are known in Hebrew (meaning owl). These were 15 S-70As built under a foreign military sale agreement between the US Army and the IAF in a contract worth US$180 million to aircraft manufacturer Sikorsky. The S-70A-50 is similiar in configuration to that of the standard US Army UH-60L, but with Israeli modifications including locally built communications and ECM systems, as well as an HH-60G rescue hoist. Israeli versions of the Black Hawk include inflight refuelling probes and stub wings for 870l (191-gallon) drop tanks. In early 1999, the IAF began a major improvement programme involving the new UH-60Ls, equipping the 15 aircraft with the aforementioned inflight refuelling probes and shoulder-mounted fuel tanks that allow easy access to the cabin and the use of cabin-mounted machine guns. Modifications were also made to the older UH-60As, including the installation of new communications, ECM, navigation, night vision and rescue systems. The summer of 2000 also saw the IAF apply a new desert camouflage scheme to several UH-60As in order to evaluate the possibility of making the normally all-black aircraft harder to detect. Although the results were said to be positive, this scheme appears no longer to be in use.

SPECIFICATIONS

Manufacturer:	*Sikorsky Aircraft*
Mission:	*multi-mission utility*
Length:	*19.5m (64ft)*
Height:	*4.8m (16ft)*
Rotor Diameter:	*16.5m (53ft)*
Crew:	*3*
Propulsion:	*2 x GE T700-701C*
Horsepower:	*3300 shaft horsepower*
Maximum Speed:	*296km/h (184mph)*
Cruise Speed:	*257km/h (160mph)*
Vertical Rate of Climb:	*472m/min (1550ft/min)*
Range:	*584km (363 miles)*
Weight:	*5224kg (11,516lb)*
Date Deployed:	*1989*
Guns:	*2 x 7.62mm machine guns*
Missiles:	*none*
Systems:	*GPS, HH-60G rescue harness*

AH-1J SEA COBRA

Built under licence by Fuji Heavy Industries, the AH-1 Sea Cobra joined the Japanese self defence forces in 1979, and 94 aircraft have been delivered since. The basic airframe design differs little from the US versions of the Cobra, but the powerplant and avionics are indigenous to Japan. The engine is manufactured by Kawasaki, and is less powerful than its US counterpart. The Japanese Cobra carries the same armament as the US version, namely the AGM-114 Hellfire missile system that provides heavy anti-armour capability for attack helicopters. The original Hellfire, such as those carried by Japanese AH-1J Cobras, are laser-guided, which means that the aircraft must remain in view of the target while the missile is in the air. This exposes the helicopter to enemy fire. The fourth-generation Longbow Hellfire is a fire-and-forget missile using a radar frequency seeker, which means the target can be acquired and engaged without the need to remain exposed. The Longbow version of the Hellfire AGMS is currently deployed only on the AH-64D Longbow Apaches, and provides a significant advantage over its predecessors. Japan's defence forces are now looking for a replacement for their ageing AH-1s, with the AH-64 Apache and the most modern Cobra heading the list.

SPECIFICATIONS

Manufacturer:	*Fuji Heavy Industries*
Mission:	*fire-support attack*
Length:	*13.9m (45ft)*
Height:	*4.4m (14ft)*
Rotor Diameter:	*14.6m (48ft)*
Crew:	*2*
Propulsion:	*2 x Kawasaki T53-K-703*
Horsepower:	*1800 shaft horsepower*
Maximum Speed:	*285km/h (178mph)*
Cruise Speed:	*227km/h (141mph)*
Vertical Rate of Climb:	*494m/min (1630ft/min)*
Range:	*507km (316 miles)*
Weight:	*2939kg (6465lb)*
Date Deployed:	*1990*
Guns:	*1 x M197 20mm turreted cannon*
Missiles:	*TOW, 40mm grenade gun, Hellfire*
Systems:	*GPS, FLIR*

CH-47J CHINOOK

The 1st Helicopter Brigade of the Japanese Ground Self-Defence Force (JGSDF) operates 32 CH-47J/JA Chinooks, manufactured locally by Kawasaki Heavy Industries (KHI) under licence from Boeing since its first delivery in 1988. The Japanese version of the Chinook resembles Britain's RAF version, with the exception of a different engine and slightly lower performance ratings. It is used for the same types of operation as in the US and Britain, generally in transportation, SAR and disaster relief operations. Kawasaki obtained two examples of the Chinook as pattern machines in 1986, and went on to build 54 more. The first five were assembled from kits supplied by Boeing. Some 40 of these CH-47Js were bought by the JGSDF, with another 16 obtained by the Japanese Air Self-Defence Force (JASDF). Later production of JGSDF Chinooks has been to CH-47JA standard. These machines are fitted with enlarged saddle tanks, nose radar, an AAQ-16 FLIR in a turret under the nose, and a partial glass cockpit. Though they are not generally configured for assault, the Japanese Chinooks could be easily pressed into frontline service if the situation called for it. Since Japan tends to take a backseat in international affairs, the CH-47J has not seen much action beyond Japanese territory, but is still invaluable to the JGSDF.

SPECIFICATIONS

Manufacturer:	*Kawasaki Heavy Industries*
Mission:	*medium support*
Length:	*15.5m (51ft)*
Height:	*5.7m (19ft)*
Rotor Diameter:	*2 x 18.3m (60ft)*
Crew:	*3/4*
Propulsion:	*2 x T55-K-712*
Horsepower:	*4333 shaft horsepower*
Maximum Speed:	*274km/h (171mph)*
Cruise Speed:	*259km/h (161mph)*
Vertical Rate of Climb:	*561m/min (1841ft/min)*
Range:	*474km (300 miles)*
Weight:	*10,814kg (23,790lb)*
Date Deployed:	*1988*
Guns:	*none*
Missiles:	*none*
Systems:	*GPS, FLIR, PNVG*

KV-107

Kawasaki's KV-107 is essentially a CH-46 Sea Knight as designed by Boeing. Following the signing of a license agreement in early 1962, Kawasaki Heavy Industries took up production of the V-107/II, as the aircraft was designated, under the model name KV-107/II. The first Kawasaki-built Sea Knight flew in May 1962. In 1965, the Japanese company signed a follow-on agreement with Boeing that allowed it to sell the helicopter on the world market. All commercial sales of the Sea Knight after that were from Kawasaki production. Thus, in many respects, the Sea Knights that operate around the world at present are essentially Japanese. The KV-107/II series was fitted with twin General Electric CT58-110-1 turboshaft engines or equivalent license-built Ishikawajima-Harima CT58-IHI-110-1 engines. Kawasaki built a number of variations of the KV-107, including a minesweeper for the Japanese Maritime Self Defence Force (JMSDF) and a troop transport version for the JGSDF. There was also a long-range SAR version, with additional fuel tanks, domed observation windows, four searchlights, a rescue hoist, plus enhanced navigation and communication electronics. Fourteen were built for the JASDF. The KV-107 helicopter has clearly been a considerable success for Kawasaki and the Japanese armed forces.

SPECIFICATIONS

Manufacturer:	*Kawasaki Heavy Industries*
Mission:	*transport, SAR*
Length:	*13.4m (44ft)*
Height:	*5.1m (17ft)*
Rotor Diameter:	*2 x 15.2m (50ft)*
Crew:	*2*
Propulsion:	*2 x CT58-IHI-110-1*
Horsepower:	*2700 shaft horsepower*
Maximum Speed:	*270km/h (168mph)*
Cruise Speed:	*250km/h (156mph)*
Vertical Rate of Climb:	*500m/min (1650ft/min)*
Range:	*441km (275 miles)*
Weight:	*5248kg (11,545lb)*
Date Deployed:	*1962*
Guns:	*none*
Missiles:	*none*
Systems:	*GPS, searchlights, winch*

OH-1 NINJA

Kawasaki designed and built the OH-1, nicknamed Ninja, as Japan's new indigenous battlefield scout helicopter. The initial prototype made its maiden flight on 6 August 1996. A total of four were delivered between May and August 1997. The JGSDF plans to purchase 180 to 200 of the OH-1s. Like similar types of light reconnaissance helicopters, the Ninja has tandem seating and stub wings for armament such as air-to-air missiles. The ducted tail rotor is of Fenestron type, in that the rotor is enclosed within the body of the tail. The design features a composite hinge-free rotor hub for high control responsibility. It also boasts damage-tolerant main rotor blades and an auto flight control system. The OH-1's targeting system is integrated, with FLIR, TV and laser ranging. The Ninja's shock-absorbing seat and crew protection armour are part of the integrated cockpit. KHI had been developing an all-composite, bearing-free helicopter main rotor system for more than 15 years. The bearing-free rotor system consists of a hub plate, torsion elements and the main rotor blades. The system is proving to be highly effective, and other variants of the OH-1 seem likely. Japan has a requirement to replace its 100 or so AH-1F Cobra attack helicopters, and one solution might be a Japanese design based on the OH-1 scout helicopter.

SPECIFICATIONS

Manufacturer:	*Kawasaki Heavy Industries*
Mission:	*reconnaissance*
Length:	*12m (39ft)*
Height:	*3.8m (12ft)*
Rotor Diameter:	*11.5m (38ft)*
Crew:	*2*
Propulsion:	*2 x Mitsubishi XT1-10*
Horsepower:	*1700 shaft horsepower*
Maximum Speed:	*260km/h (162mph)*
Cruise Speed:	*200km/h (125mph)*
Vertical Rate of Climb:	*not available*
Range:	*550km (344mph)*
Weight:	*2500kg (5500lb)*
Date Deployed:	*1997*
Guns:	*none*
Missiles:	*air-to-air missiles*
Systems:	*GPS, FLIR, laser rangefinder*

S-80M SEA DRAGON

The JMSDF S-80 Sea Dragon helicopter is used primarily for Airborne Mine Countermeasures (AMCM), with a secondary mission of shipboard delivery. The large aircraft is capable of carrying up to 55 troops or a 16-ton payload. It is also capable of towing a variety of minesweeping countermeasure systems, including the Mk 105 minesweeping sled, the AQS-14 side-scan sonar, and the Mk 103 mechanical minesweeping system. Since Japan is heavily reliant on imports for almost all of its energy and food, keeping open the vital shipping lanes is crucial. Thus the S-80 Sea Dragon, which is virtually identical to the US Navy's MH-53E, is charged with the task of keeping Japan's sea lanes free of mines, both during war and in peacetime. To achieve its goals, AMCM missions include minesweeping and ancillary spotting, mine neutralization, floating mine destruction, channel marking and surface towing of small craft and ships. For AMCM missions, the S-80 helicopter is operated by a crew of seven, comprising pilot, copilot, safety observer, port and starboard AMCM equipment handlers, and port and starboard ramp operators. The S-80 Sea Dragon can be refuelled inflight, as well as at the hover, which allows it to remain airborne for longer, thus extending its operational effectiveness.

SPECIFICATIONS

Manufacturer:	Sikorsky Aircraft
Mission:	heavy transport, minesweeping
Length:	30m (99ft)
Height:	8.5m (28ft)
Rotor Diameter:	24m (79ft)
Crew:	3/4
Propulsion:	3 x GE T64
Horsepower:	13,500 shaft horsepower
Maximum Speed:	315km/h (195mph)
Cruise Speed:	278km/h (172mph)
Vertical Rate of Climb:	420m/min (1386ft/min)
Range:	889km (550 miles)
Weight:	15,070kg (33,226lb)
Date Deployed:	1981
Guns:	2 x .50in machine guns
Missiles:	none
Systems:	GPS, FLIR, acoustic sensors, MAD

SH-60J SEAHAWK

Japan's self defence forces have contracted the SH-60J as a replacement for their ageing SH-3 Sea King ASW helicopter. Mitsubishi was selected to manufacture the SH-60J under licence from Sikorsky. While the basic airframe design is almost entirely from the original US-built S-70 Black Hawk (upon which the SH-60J is based), much of the helicopter is an indigenous Japanese design. The avionics are entirely Japanese, with the exception of the AN/APS-124 radar. The SH-60J first flew in Japanese service in August 1987. It is now in the process of replacing the elderly JMSDF-operated Sea Kings. Although used primarily as a patrol helicopter, operating onboard Japanese warships such as the Shirane or Haruna class ASW destroyers, the SH-60J can be configured to carry the necessary equipment to become an anti-submarine or anti-ship helicopter, in the same mould as the US Navy SH-60B Seahawk. While the SH-60J has never been deployed in war, it is on constant alert for unwanted intruders, with North Korean spy boats generally the prime suspects. The successful H-60 airframe from Sikorsky has shown itself to be the favourite for armed forces the world over. As a result, the Japanese Defence Agency (JDA) has ordered more of the MHI SH-60Js to replace its outdated HSS-2B aircraft.

SPECIFICATIONS

Manufacturer:	Mitsubishi Heavy Industries
Mission:	patrol
Length:	15.3m (50ft)
Height:	3.8m (13ft)
Rotor Diameter:	16.4m (54ft)
Crew:	3
Propulsion:	2 x GE T700-401C
Horsepower:	3400 shaft horsepower
Maximum Speed:	296km/h (184mph)
Cruise Speed:	250km/h (155mph)
Vertical Rate of Climb:	545m/min (1800ft/min)
Range:	833km (518 miles)
Weight:	6191kg (13,650lb)
Date Deployed:	1987
Guns:	none
Missiles:	none
Systems:	GPS, AN/APS-124 radar

SUPER LYNX

The latest generation of Lynx helicopters, the Super Lynx 300, took its maiden flight in June 2001. The first production version (for the Malaysian Navy) flew in May 2002. It incorporates an all-new glass cockpit with seven-colour active matrix liquid crystal displays (LCDs), new avionics, improved airframe, more powerful CTS800-4N engines (jointly developed by Rolls-Royce and the Honeywell partnership, LHTEC) with Full Authority Digital Electronic Control (FADEC). The new engines will operate more effectively in hot and humid conditions. A version of the Super Lynx 300, known as Future Lynx, is also to be developed to replace the British Army's Mk 7 and Mk 9 Lynx helicopters. The Lynx airframe is constructed of composite and light alloy. The non-retractable tricycle-type landing gear is designed for the helicopter to operate from small ships in high seas, and features oleo-pneumatic struts which absorb the shock of a 2m/sec (6ft/sec) descent rate. A hydraulically operated harpoon deck lock secures the helicopter to the deck. It is equipped with the Sea Skua, an all-weather anti-ship missile developed by Matra BAe Dynamics to provide medium- and long-range defence. Countries deploying the Sea Skua missile include Britain, Bahrain, Germany, South Korea, Brazil and Turkey. The Lynx carries four Sea Skua missiles.

SPECIFICATIONS

Manufacturer:	*Westland Helicopters*
Mission:	*naval multi-role*
Length:	*13.5m (44ft)*
Height:	*3.7m (12ft)*
Rotor Diameter:	*12.8m (42ft)*
Crew:	*2*
Propulsion:	*2 x Rolls-Royce/LHTEC CTS800-4N*
Horsepower:	*1800 shaft horsepower*
Maximum Speed:	*259km/h (161mph)*
Cruise Speed:	*225km/h (140mph)*
Vertical Rate of Climb:	*600m/min (1994ft/min)*
Range:	*590km (368 miles)*
Weight:	*3291kg (7240lb)*
Date Deployed:	*2002*
Guns:	*none*
Missiles:	*Sea Skua, depth charges, torpedoes*
Systems:	*Sea Spray radar, thermal imager*

KA-25 HORMONE

The deployment of the Polaris naval strategic nuclear missile system in the US acted as a catalyst that accelerated the development of aircraft-carrying ships in the former USSR. The KA-25 Hormone helicopter was developed to meet a Soviet Naval Air Force (SNAF) specification for an anti-submarine helicopter for ship- or shore-based use. The first KA-25 prototype flew in 1961. Designed by the world's leading pioneer of co-axial helicopters, Nikolai I. Kamov (1902–73), this Soviet AV-MF (naval aviation) ASW aircraft was assigned to the Soviet helicopter carrier *Moskva*. The KA-25 Hormone is powered by twin turbine engines – installed side-by-side above the cabin – which drive two three-bladed coaxial, contra-rotating rotors. The contra-rotating rotors eliminate the need for an anti-torque tail rotor. This makes a very compact design possible, with obvious benefits for shipboard operations. While still an effective aircraft, the Hormone was deployed more than 30 years ago and is now getting a little long in the tooth. One major drawback of the design is that the helicopter cannot hover or dip at night. This gives the Hormone's competitors a distinct advantage. However, the helicopter is still in widespread use, even though it has generally been superseded by more advanced and capable ASW aircraft.

SPECIFICATIONS

Manufacturer:	*Kamov Company*
Mission:	*ASW, reconnaissance*
Length:	*9.8m (32 ft)*
Height:	*5.4m (17ft)*
Rotor Diameter:	*15.7m (52ft)*
Crew:	*2*
Propulsion:	*2 x Glushnekov GTD-3*
Horsepower:	*1700 shaft horsepower*
Maximum Speed:	*220km/h (137mph)*
Cruise Speed:	*195km/h (121mph)*
Vertical Rate of Climb:	*not available*
Range:	*400km (250 miles)*
Weight:	*7100kg (16,100lb)*
Date Deployed:	*1970*
Guns:	*none*
Missiles:	*E45-75A torpedo*
Systems:	*dipping sonar, 3 sonobuoys, MAD*

KA-28 HELIX

NATO calls it the Helix, while its official designation is the Ka-28 naval anti-submarine helicopter, designed and manufactured by the Kamov Company in Russia. More than 60 Ka-27/28s are in service in Russia. The helicopters have also been exported to Cuba, India, Syria, Vietnam and the former Yugoslavia. The mission of these helicopters is to detect, track and destroy submerged submarines at depths of up to 500m (1640ft) and running at speeds up to 75km/h (47mph) at any time of the year and in all weather conditions. The Ka-28 has both day and night operations capability. It is equipped with a radar system for navigation and to detect surfaced submarines and responder beacons. The VGS-3 dipping sonar detects submarines, determines their coordinates and transfers the data in semi-automatic mode to data transmission equipment. The mission computer carries out automatic control, stabilization and guidance of the helicopter. The aircraft is also MAD-equipped and has an airborne receiver to detect and guide it towards sonobuoy radio transmissions. The export version Ka-28 also has an Identification Friend or Foe (IFF) system. The helicopter is armed with one homing torpedo, one torpedo rocket, 10 PLAB 250lb anti-submarine bombs and two OMAB marine marking bombs.

SPECIFICATIONS

Manufacturer:	Kamov Company
Mission:	ASW
Length:	12.2m (40ft)
Height:	5.4m (18ft)
Rotor Diameter:	15.9m (52ft)
Crew:	2
Propulsion:	2 x TV3-117V
Horsepower:	4000 shaft horsepower
Maximum Speed:	280km/h (175mph)
Cruise Speed:	240km/h (150mph)
Vertical Rate of Climb:	350m/min (1155ft/min)
Range:	450km (281 miles)
Weight:	5520kg (12,144lb)
Date Deployed:	1985
Guns:	2 x 7.62mm machine guns
Missiles:	torpedoes, PLAB, OMAB bombs
Systems:	MAD, VGS-3 dipping sonar

KA-29 HELIX B

Kamov's Ka-29 is the naval combat and transport helicopter version of the Ka-27. The mission of the aircraft is to land navy and infantry units from combatant ships and to ensure fire-support for seaborne assault troops. The helicopter can also ferry personnel and cargo from bases, and supply vessels to combatant ships. The Ka-29 is powered by two TV3-117V turboshaft engines. Its basic structure is very similar to that of the Ka-27 and Ka-28, and it can be re-equipped while on the assembly line. Transport and combat versions can be produced during assembly at the manufacturing plant, while the variants can also be changed in the field. The cargo cabin accommodates at least two tons of supplies or 16 armed troops. For casualty evacuation, it can carry four stretcher patients and seven seated wounded, with one medical attendant. According to the mission requirements, the helicopter can be armed with rockets, bombs and machine-gun pods mounted on the weapon pylons on both sides of the fuselage. Bombs and containers can be also arranged in the helicopter's torpedo bay. The helicopter is fitted with a 7.62mm flexibly mounted machine gun with 1800 rounds. A number of measures are taken to increase combat survivability, including armour protection. The Ka-29 has been in service with the Russian Armed Forces since 1985.

SPECIFICATIONS

Manufacturer:	Kamov Company
Mission:	naval combat, transport
Length:	12.2m (40ft)
Height:	5.4m (18ft)
Rotor Diameter:	15.9m (52ft)
Crew:	2
Propulsion:	2 x Isotov TV3-117V
Horsepower:	4000 shaft horsepower
Maximum Speed:	280km/h (175mph)
Cruise Speed:	240km/h (150mph)
Vertical Rate of Climb:	350m/min (1155ft/min)
Range:	450km (281 miles)
Weight:	5520kg (12,144lb)
Date Deployed:	1985
Guns:	1 x 7.62mm machine gun
Missiles:	rockets, bombs, torpedoes
Systems:	GPS

KA-32

The Ka-32 helicopter is intended for long-range detection of other aircraft, whether fixed or rotary wing. It is designed to find and track air targets at high or low altitudes and over water. It then transmits data automatically to the command posts. The helicopter can increase considerably the combat mission efficiency of all force elements by providing them with timely information about enemy air movements. Kamov's Ka-32 is developed from the basic Ka-27 ship-borne coaxial helicopter, taking its essential features and tailoring the equipment to suit its specialized mission. Under the transport cabin floor there is a compartment housing the support mechanism of a 6m (20ft)-span rotating antenna. The submarine search and attack equipment of the Ka-27 has been removed; instead, a radio-electronic suite is installed for radar target detection, target identification and transmission of the situation data to ship- and ground-based command posts. The radio-electronic package automatically controls the helicopter flight over the specified route in any climatic conditions. When the radio-electronic package is on, the antenna is extended and the navigator has selected the operational mode, all further operations are performed automatically without operator interference. Ka-32 helicopters are based aboard ships and at land locations.

SPECIFICATIONS

Manufacturer:	*Kamov Company*
Mission:	*AEW*
Length:	*11.3m (37ft)*
Height:	*5.4m (18ft)*
Rotor Diameter:	*15.9m (52ft)*
Crew:	*2*
Propulsion:	*2 x Isotov TV3-117V*
Horsepower:	*4000 shaft horsepower*
Maximum Speed:	*280km/h (175mph)*
Cruise Speed:	*235km/h (146mph)*
Vertical Rate of Climb:	*924m/min (3050ft/min)*
Range:	*460km (287 miles)*
Weight:	*5520kg (12,170lb)*
Date Deployed:	*1995*
Guns:	*1 x 7.62mm machine gun*
Missiles:	*AT-6, rockets*
Systems:	*E-801 OKO 360-degree radar*

KA-50 HOKUM

The Ka-50 Hokum, nicknamed Werewolf or Black Shark, is a powerful, state-of-the-art battle helicopter in limited service with the Russian Air Force. There are two versions. The Ka-50 Hokum is a single-seat, close-support aircraft and is competing to fulfil the Russian Army Aviation requirement for a night-capable anti-tank helicopter, a replacement for the 25-year-old Mi-24. The helicopter has a number of special features, including its single seat to improve combat and flight characteristics and reduce operational costs. It was designed for remote operations, with no need of ground maintenance facilities for two weeks at a time. The fully armoured pilot's cabin can withstand 23mm gunfire. The pilot ejection system functions at any height and allows successful ejection at low altitude and maximum speed. A typical mix for targeting armour formations is 12x AT-16 ATGMs, 500 x 30mm cannon rounds and two 20-round pods of 80mm FFAR. It also carries guided air-to-air missiles. The Hokum's most remarkable feature is a remote targeting system that can facilitate an effective attack from a distance that rules out direct visual contact with the target. However, as with much of the recent Russian military procurement programme, the Ka-50 development has suffered due to lack of funds and may never see widespread service.

SPECIFICATIONS

Manufacturer:	*Kamov Company*
Mission:	*attack*
Length:	*15m (50ft)*
Height:	*4.9m (16ft)*
Rotor Diameter:	*14.5m (48ft)*
Crew:	*1*
Propulsion:	*2 x Klimov TV3*
Horsepower:	*4000 shaft horsepower*
Maximum Speed:	*340km/h (212mph)*
Cruise Speed:	*290km/h (181mph)*
Vertical Rate of Climb:	*600m/min (1980ft/min)*
Range:	*460km (290 miles)*
Weight:	*7692kg (16,922lb)*
Date Deployed:	*2000*
Guns:	*1 x 2A42 30mm cannon*
Missiles:	*AT-16, 80mm rockets, AA-11*
Systems:	*FLIR, TV or thermal sight, PNVG*

KA-52 ALLIGATOR

Nicknamed Alligator, the Ka-52 is the second version of the Ka-50 in limited service with the Russian Air Force. It is a twin-seat, close-support helicopter that is also used as a trainer for the single-seat Ka-50. The helicopter has two pilots who sit side-by-side rather than one behind the other, and is therefore heavier than its single-seat counterpart. Performance is marginally reduced as a result. The Ka-52 is intended for a wide range of combat tasks in daytime and night conditions. It can operate in most weather conditions and has the same capabilities as the Ka-50. The Ka-52 helicopter differs through a wider nose part and the side-by-side, twin-seat crew cockpit. Both pilots have full control of the helicopter without any limitations. Numerous weapon options are achieved by arranging a movable, high-speed firing gun starboard of the helicopter, and by six external wing stores with different combinations of anti-tank missiles, rockets, air-to-air missiles and bombs. The Alligator is comparable with the Werewolf helicopter in terms of weaponry, if not weight, and is a match for most existing combat helicopters. However, as with the Ka-50, there is serious doubt about whether the Ka-52 will see any kind of widespread deployment within Russia's armed forces for reasons of cost and inefficiency in the post-Soviet era.

SPECIFICATIONS

Manufacturer:	Kamov Company
Mission:	attack
Length:	15m (50ft)
Height:	4.6m (15ft)
Rotor Diameter:	14.5m (48ft)
Crew:	2
Propulsion:	2 x Klimov TV3
Horsepower:	4000 shaft horsepower
Maximum Speed:	330km/h (206mph)
Cruise Speed:	279km/h (174mph)
Vertical Rate of Climb:	600m/min (1980ft/min)
Range:	460km (290 miles)
Weight:	7930kg (17,446lb)
Date Deployed:	2000
Guns:	1 x 2A42 30mm cannon
Missiles:	AT-16, 80mm rockets, AA-11
Systems:	FLIR, TV or thermal sight, PNVG

KA-60 KASATKA

Known as the Killer Whale, the Ka-60 Kasatka is a medium-weight transport helicopter developed by Kamov. Aircraft from Kamov are best known for their coaxial contra-rotating rotor design, but the Ka-60 has a single four-bladed main rotor with an anti-torque tail rotor. The Ka-60 is intended as a replacement for the outmoded Mi-8 in the Russian military, offering a 60 percent saving in fuel consumption as well as far superior reliability and maintainability. It is to fulfil a wide variety of roles, from training and troop transport to all-weather reconnaissance and target designation for attack helicopters. The Ka-60 is designed for carrying troops, weapons and ammunition to the battlefield, evacuation of casualties and cargo transport using the external hook. Kamov first unveiled the Ka-60 helicopter in 1997, and its first flight took place in 1998. The helicopter went on international display at the MAKS 1999 show held in Moscow. Kamov has announced that production will start in 2003 at the RSK MiG Lukhovitsky machine-building plant near Moscow. As well as the Ka-60 transport, Kamov has developed a civilian utility variant, the Ka-62. More so than other Russian developments in helicopter design, the Ka-60 has a real chance of success. Away from Russia's sphere of influence, though, it faces stiff opposition from other makers.

SPECIFICATIONS

Manufacturer:	Kamov Company
Mission:	medium transport
Length:	13.5m (45ft)
Height:	3.8m (13ft)
Rotor Diameter:	13.5m (45ft)
Crew:	2
Propulsion:	2 x RD-600V
Horsepower:	2400 shaft horsepower
Maximum Speed:	300km/h (187mph)
Cruise Speed:	275km/h (171mph)
Vertical Rate of Climb:	624m/min (2059ft/min)
Range:	625km (390 miles)
Weight:	6000kg (13,200lb)
Date Deployed:	2000
Guns:	2x 7.62mm machine gun
Missiles:	80mm rockets
Systems:	GPS, Arbalet radar

MI-2 HOPLITE

The elderly Mi-2 Hoplite provides transport and fire-support services. The helicopter can conduct reconnaissance, re-supply guerrillas and provide close air support with 57mm rockets. It can also have a smoke generator mounted to provide a wide-area smokescreen in front of ground units, screening their movements. Additional missions include direct air support, anti-tank, armed reconnaissance, transport, medevac, airborne command post, mine-laying and training. Although the Mi-2 Hoplite was developed by the Mil bureau in the former Soviet Union, the aircraft was produced exclusively in Poland by the WSK-PZL Swidnik aircraft factory. Several thousand of these aircraft were built, and they remained in production until 1985. The cabin door is hinged rather than sliding, which can limit operations. There is no armour protection for the cockpit or cabin. Ammunition storage is in the aircraft cabin, so combat load varies by mission. Some Mi-2s currently employ fuselage-mounted weapon racks rather than the standard 23mm fuselage-mounted cannon. Other variants employ the cannon. Although production has now ceased, the Mi-2 Hoplite still operates successfully in more than 20 countries, though generally in more of a paramilitary or law enforcement role, rather than in a frontline military capacity.

SPECIFICATIONS

Manufacturer:	Mil/PZL Swidnik
Mission:	transport, cargo, reconnaissance
Length:	11.9m (39ft)
Height:	3.7m (12ft)
Rotor Diameter:	14.6m (47ft)
Crew:	1/2
Propulsion:	2 x PZL GTD-350
Horsepower:	760 shaft horsepower
Maximum Speed:	220km/h (137mph)
Cruise Speed:	194km/h (121mph)
Vertical Rate of Climb:	270m/min (891ft/min)
Range:	580km (362 miles)
Weight:	2372kg (5218lb)
Date Deployed:	1965
Guns:	23mm cannon
Missiles:	AT-3, SA-7, 57mm rockets
Systems:	GPS, basic flight systems

MI-8 HIP

The Mi-8 Hip is a highly successful multi-role transport helicopter capable of carrying troops or supplies as well as conducting armed attacks with rockets and guns. Introduced as a replacement for the Mi-4 Hound, it is often used to re-supply guerrillas, insert troops or provide close air support to attacking units. Designed as a transport helicopter, the Mi-8 proved to be a versatile machine capable of carrying large cargo sizes weighing up to three tons. If required, it can become both combat, rescue and artillery observation helicopter, accommodating three crew. The first Mi-8 flew in January 1960, and by 1985 more than 1500 had been built. The success of this helicopter has seen it become the base design for the export version Mi-17 and the naval Mi-14. It has been exported to dozens of countries and seen plenty of combat. The survivability features of the Mi-8 include crew cabin armour plating, explosive-resistant foam filling in the fuel tanks, a fire-fighting system, plus duplicated and back-up hydraulics, power systems and main control circuits. An SAR version was developed from the military transport helicopter. In rescue missions, the helicopter crew drop radio-beacons to mark the distress area and deliver rescue teams to aid and recover the casualties.

SPECIFICATIONS

Manufacturer:	Mil Helicopter Factory
Mission:	armed transport
Length:	18.4m (61ft)
Height:	5.7m (19ft)
Rotor Diameter:	21.3m (70ft)
Crew:	3
Propulsion:	2 x Isotov TV3-117
Horsepower:	3500 shaft horsepower
Maximum Speed:	240km/h (150mph)
Cruise Speed:	225km/h (140mph)
Vertical Rate of Climb:	540m/min (1782ft/min)
Range:	495km (309 miles)
Weight:	7200kg (15,840lb)
Date Deployed:	1981
Guns:	2 x 7.62mm machine guns
Missiles:	AT-2, AT-3, 57mm rockets
Systems:	autopilot, PNVG, infrared jammer

MI-14 HAZE

A shore-based naval version of the Mi-8 Hip, the Mi-14 Haze has a boat-shaped bottom and fully retractable undercarriage, enabling it to land on water. The aircraft can be fitted with ASW equipment, with a radome under the nose and MAD mounted under the tail boom. It is equally happy in SAR or mine-sweeping roles. In addition to its multi-role capability, the Mi-14 features high flight performance, boasting a maximum 1135km (709 mile) range. Currently, its only real competitor is the Eurocopter AS 332L1 Super Puma. When functioning in its SAR guise, the Mi-14 Haze can land on water, drop up to 20 liferafts overboard and accommodate at least 20 survivors. The Haze is similar to the Mi-8 in terms of the fuselage, but with the addition of the boat hull. The engines are the same Isotov turboshafts as those fitted to the Mi-24 Hind gunship series. Rescue versions do not typically carry any armament, but do have a 500kg (1102lb) capacity winch above the side door. The Mi-14PL is the ASW version, while the minesweeper is designated Mi-14BT and the Mi-14PS is the SAR derivative. The Haze has been exported very successfully by Russia, and is currently operated by Bulgaria, Cuba, Ethiopia, North Korea, Poland, Romania, Syria and the former Yugoslavia.

SPECIFICATIONS

Manufacturer:	*Mil Helicopter Factory*
Mission:	*SAR, ASW*
Length:	*25.3m (83ft)*
Height:	*6.9m (22ft)*
Rotor Diameter:	*21.3m (70ft)*
Crew:	*3*
Propulsion:	*2 x Isotov TV3-117*
Horsepower:	*3354 shaft horsepower*
Maximum Speed:	*230km/h (143mph)*
Cruise Speed:	*215km/h (134mph)*
Vertical Rate of Climb:	*not available*
Range:	*1135km (709 miles)*
Weight:	*9000kg (19,800lb)*
Date Deployed:	*not available*
Guns:	*none*
Missiles:	*E45-75A torpedo, depth charges*
Systems:	*MAD, dipping sonar, sonobuoys*

MI-17 HIP H

The Mi-17 is a multi-role helicopter derivative of the Russian Mi-8 Hip, and can be used to re-supply or insert troop detachments. It can also be very heavily armed with an extensive array of rockets, missiles and guns. It is often used by air assault infantry forces to attack the point of penetration, reinforce units in contact or disrupt counterattacks. Additional missions include attack, direct air support, electronic warfare, AEW, medevac, SAR and minelaying. The Mi-17 is manufactured at the Kazan Helicopter Production Association for export. The Russian armed forces call it Mi-8MT. The Mi-17 can be recognized because it has the tail rotor at the starboard side, instead of at the port side. It is capable of carrying cargo in the cabin with half-open or removed doors, plus external loads or passengers. Up to 30 armed troops and up to 20 wounded can also be accommodated. The aircraft can be used for in-flight unloading of special cargoes. The Mi-17 is provided with missiles, bombs, small arms and cannon. It may be equipped with long-range communication equipment and radar. In addition, it can carry equipment with phased-array antennae for suppression of enemy electronic attack and neutralization of air defence facilities such as surface-to-air-missile (SAM) sites.

SPECIFICATIONS

Manufacturer:	Mil/Kazan
Mission:	armed multi-role
Length:	18.4m (61ft)
Height:	5.7m (19ft)
Rotor Diameter:	21.3m (70ft)
Crew:	3
Propulsion:	2 x Isotov TV3-117MT
Horsepower:	4000 shaft horsepower
Maximum Speed:	250km/h (156mph)
Cruise Speed:	240km/h (150mph)
Vertical Rate of Climb:	540m/min (1782ft/min)
Range:	495km (309 miles)
Weight:	7200kg (15,840lb)
Date Deployed:	1981
Guns:	2 x 7.62mm machine guns
Missiles:	rockets, missiles, bombs
Systems:	autopilot, PNVG, infrared jammer

MI-24 HIND

Feared on the battlefield, the Mi-24 Hind is a versatile attack helicopter with transport capabilities.

Developed around the Mi-8 Hip's propulsion system, it was the first helicopter to enter service with the Russian Air Force as an assault transport and gunship. Other missions include direct air support, anti-tank, armed escort and air combat. The helicopter was used extensively in the Russia/Afghanistan war, becoming the signature weapon of the conflict. The Mi-24 is a close counterpart to the US Apache but, unlike this and other Western attack helicopters, it is also capable of transporting up to eight troops. Able to carry different types of ammunition, a typical armament make-up would be eight AT-6 ATGMs, 750x 30mm rounds, plus two 57mm rocket pods. The Hind can store additional ammunition in the cargo compartment in lieu of troops. Armoured cockpits and a titanium rotor head are able to withstand 20mm cannon hits. Every aircraft has an overpressurization system for operation in a nuclear, bacteriological or chemical (NBC) environment. Because of problems with their flight characteristics, which can leave them temporarily vulnerable to more nimble aircraft, they usually attack in pairs or groups from various directions. This negates any weakness from which a single aircraft might suffer.

SPECIFICATIONS

Manufacturer:	Mil Helicopter Factory
Mission:	attack, transport
Length:	18.5m (61ft)
Height:	6.5m (21ft)
Rotor Diameter:	17.3m (57ft)
Crew:	2
Propulsion:	2 x Isotov TV3-117
Horsepower:	4450 shaft horsepower
Maximum Speed:	335km/h (210mph)
Cruise Speed:	295km/h (185mph)
Vertical Rate of Climb:	750m/min (2460ft/min)
Range:	495km (309 miles)
Weight:	8500kg (18,700lb)
Date Deployed:	1976
Guns:	1 x 12.7mm chain gun
Missiles:	AT-6, 57mm rockets, AA-8 Aphid
Systems:	FLIR, RWR, laser designator

MI-26 HALO

The Mi-26 Halo is the heaviest and most powerful helicopter in the world, designed to carry large-size cargoes weighing up to 20.3 tonnes (20 tons). It is the result of an early 1970s specification for a transport helicopter whose empty weight, without fuel, was not to exceed half of its maximum take-off weight. It can be used for construction projects ranging from bridges to power transmission lines. The combination of high load-carrying capacity and high cruise speed makes the use of the helicopter economically efficient. The Halo has no armament. The load and lift capabilities of the aircraft are comparable to those of the US C-130 Hercules transport aircraft. The Halo has a closed-circuit television (CCTV) system to observe positioning over a sling load, and to monitor load operations. The Mi-26 has some variants including a medevac version, a freight transporter and a fuel tanker. It is an awesome aircraft, and has seen action all over the world, taking part in Russia's war in Afghanistan. It has been exported to many other nations, including India and most of the former Soviet republics. It is capable of carrying 100 troops as well as armoured vehicles. It is still in operation and, on occasion, is hired by Western nations that require a heavy-lift helicopter to transport equipment into areas that a normal fixed-wing aircraft cannot reach.

SPECIFICATIONS

Manufacturer:	Mil Helicopter Factory
Mission:	heavy transport
Length:	33.5m (110ft)
Height:	8.1m (26ft)
Rotor Diameter:	32m (105ft)
Crew:	5
Propulsion:	2 x Lotarev D-136
Horsepower:	22,300 shaft horsepower
Maximum Speed:	295km/h (184mph)
Cruise Speed:	255km/h (159mph)
Vertical Rate of Climb:	not available
Range:	800km (500 miles)
Weight:	28,200kg (62,040lb)
Date Deployed:	1983
Guns:	none
Missiles:	none
Systems:	internal auto-loading system

MI-28 HAVOC

K nown by the NATO codename Havoc, the Mi-28 combat helicopter is a rival to the Ka-50 Hokum, or Werewolf. The new Mil design is based on the conventional pod and boom configuration with a tail rotor. An innovative design of all-plastic rotor blades, which can survive hits from 30mm cannon shells, has been installed on the Night Havoc Mi-28N version. Engines are two TV3-117 turboshafts, providing high speed and reasonable range. Energy-absorbing landing gear and seats protect the crew in a crash landing or in a low-altitude vertical fall. The two crew members are able to survive a vertical fall of up to 12m/sec (39ft/sec). The Mi-28N Night Havoc is armed with Shturm and Ataka anti-tank missiles. The former weapon is radio command guided, while the latter has a radar guidance system and considerably longer range. Up to 16 anti-tank missiles can be mounted on the aircraft. The helicopter can also carry four containers each with 20x 80mm unguided rockets or with five 122mm rockets. The Havoc is equipped with a turreted 2A42 30mm cannon. The pilot uses a helmet-mounted target designator, which allocates the target to the navigator's surveillance and fire control system. The navigator/weapons officer is then able to deploy guided weapons or the gun against the target.

SPECIFICATIONS

Manufacturer:	*Mil Helicopter Factory*
Mission:	*attack*
Length:	*17m (56ft)*
Height:	*3.8m (13ft)*
Rotor Diameter:	*17.2m (57ft)*
Crew:	*2*
Propulsion:	*2 x Isotov TV3-117VMA*
Horsepower:	*4000 shaft horsepower*
Maximum Speed:	*324km/h (202mph)*
Cruise Speed:	*265km/h (165mph)*
Vertical Rate of Climb:	*810m/min (2675ft/min)*
Range:	*460km (287 miles)*
Weight:	*7890kg (17,358lb)*
Date Deployed:	*2001*
Guns:	*1 x 2A42 30mm cannon*
Missiles:	*Shturm, Ataka*
Systems:	*GPS, FLIR, terrain-following radar*

AH-2 ROOIVALK

The Rooivalk is a latest-generation attack helicopter from Denel Aviation of South Africa. It has completed the development, test and evaluation phase and entered full-scale production. The South African Air Force (SAAF) has ordered 16 Rooivalk AH-2s for two squadrons, the first of which entered service in July 1999. The Rooivalk has a crash-resistant structure and is designed for stealth with low radar, visual, infrared and acoustic signatures. It carries a comprehensive range of weaponry selected for the mission requirement, ranging from anti-armour and anti-helicopter missions to ground suppression and ferry duties. The aircraft can engage multiple targets at short and long range, utilizing the nose-mounted cannon and a range of underwing-mounted munitions. Denel is developing the Mokopa anti-tank missile for the Rooivalk. Mokopa has either a semi-active laser or millimetre wave radar seeker head, and is equipped with a tandem warhead. Range is more than 8km (5 miles). Rooivalk can also fire Hellfire or HOT 3 missiles, and can carry four air-to-air missiles such as the Kentron V3C Darter or MBDA Mistral. The Rooivalk's electronic warfare suite is the fully integrated Helicopter Electronic Warfare Self-Protection Suite (HEWSS), incorporating radar warning, laser warning and countermeasures.

SPECIFICATIONS

Manufacturer:	*Denel Aviation*
Mission:	*attack*
Length:	*18.7m (62ft)*
Height:	*5.1m (17ft)*
Rotor Diameter:	*15.6m (51ft)*
Crew:	*2*
Propulsion:	*2 x GTE Makila 1K2*
Horsepower:	*not available*
Maximum Speed:	*371km/h (231mph)*
Cruise Speed:	*278km/h (173mph)*
Vertical Rate of Climb:	*798m/min (2633ft/min)*
Range:	*700km (438 miles)*
Weight:	*5730kg (12,606lb)*
Date Deployed:	*1999*
Guns:	*1 x 20mm cannon*
Missiles:	*ATM Mokopa, Hellfire, FFAR*
Systems:	*GPS, FLIR, HUD*

DENEL ORYX

Atlas Denel's Oryx helicopter is the South African National Defence Force version of the SA 330B Puma. It shares many of the same characteristics, but has had a number of modifications made to it in order to improve performance in South Africa's more demanding climate. Such improvements include filters for the air intakes which prevent sand and dust getting into the engines. Also, the aircraft has been modified to make operating in the heat of South Africa's inner territories more practical. In its operational roles, the Oryx can carry up to 20 fully armed combat troops, or six stretchers for medical evacuation. The South African armed forces have embarked on a modernization drive to improve their fighting abilities, and integration of the Oryx helicopter into troop manoeuvre and deployment has been central to this process. Indeed, South Africa recently took part in a joint training exercise with the US where Oryx helicopters were used to evacuate dozens of casualties to a mobile field hospital. The Oryx replaced the older Eurocopter Puma that the air force had been using since the 1970s. Though the new Oryx is essentially a Eurocopter AS 332 Super Puma, the extensive modifications made to the basic design by the two South African companies Atlas and Denel make it a very different beast to its European counterparts.

SPECIFICATIONS

Manufacturer:	*Atlas Denel*
Mission:	*utility transport*
Length:	*15.5m (51ft)*
Height:	*4.9m (16ft)*
Rotor Diameter:	*15m (49ft)*
Crew:	*2*
Propulsion:	*2 x Turbomeca Makila*
Horsepower:	*3500 shaft horsepower*
Maximum Speed:	*271km/h (169mph)*
Cruise Speed:	*258km/h (161mph)*
Vertical Rate of Climb:	*420m/min (1386ft/min)*
Range:	*850km (531 miles)*
Weight:	*4370kg (9614lb)*
Date Deployed:	*1992*
Guns:	*2 x 7.62 machine guns*
Missiles:	*none*
Systems:	*GPS*

AH-1W SUPER COBRA

The Bell AH-1W Super Cobra is a day/night marginal-weather US Marine Corps (USMC) attack helicopter that provides en-route escort for assault helicopters and their embarked forces. The AH-1W is a two-crew, tandem-seat, twin-engine helicopter capable of land- or sea-based operations. It provides fire support and fire support coordination to the landing force during amphibious assaults and subsequent operations ashore. The original AH-1 Cobra was conceived and built during the 1960s, and saw action in the Vietnam War. It has gone through a number of changes over the years, with the newest incarnation, the AH-1Z, currently in development. It is a testament to the vision of the original design concept that the twenty-first century model bears more than a passing resemblance to its less technologically advanced predecessors, given the pace of development and fierce competition in the attack helicopter marketplace. While the AH-1 Cobra is in service with armed forces the world over in its various guises, the Super Cobra represents the pinnacle of AH-1 development. This helicopter has served with great distinction in many of the late twentieth century's conflicts, including the Gulf War, the Balkans and most recently in Afghanistan. The Super Cobra's potent arsenal of advanced weaponry gives it a distinct advantage on the modern battlefield.

SPECIFICATIONS

Manufacturer:	*Bell Helicopter Textron*
Mission:	*close-support attack*
Length:	*13.9m (45ft)*
Height:	*4.4m (14ft)*
Rotor Diameter:	*14.6m (48ft)*
Crew:	*2*
Propulsion:	*2 x GE T700-401*
Horsepower:	*2082 shaft horsepower*
Maximum Speed:	*313km/h (195mph)*
Cruise Speed:	*278km/h (173mph)*
Vertical Rate of Climb:	*583m/min (1925ft/min)*
Range:	*470km (294 miles)*
Weight:	*4634kg (10,194lb)*
Date Deployed:	*1986*
Guns:	*1 x M-197 20mm turreted cannon*
Missiles:	*Hellfire, Sidewinder, Sidearm*
Systems:	*Kollsman night target system*

AH-64D APACHE

Boeing's (McDonnell Douglas) AH-64 Apache is the US Army's primary attack helicopter. It is a fast, quick-reacting, airborne weapon system. The Apache is designed to fight and survive during the day, night and in adverse weather conditions. The principal mission is the destruction of high-value targets with the Hellfire missile. It is also capable of employing a 30mm M230 chain gun and Hydra 70mm (2.75in) rockets that are effective against a wide variety of targets. The Apache has a full range of aircraft survivability equipment, and has the ability to withstand hits in critical areas from rounds of up to 23mm. The AH-64D variation of the Apache, introduced in 1998, is the latest addition and incorporates the state-of-the-art Longbow radar system. This enables it to locate, designate and prioritize battlefield targets, disseminate the information to other aircraft in the area, and then initiate a precision attack. These targets can be engaged and destroyed from a distance of up to 8km (5 miles). The AH-64D further enhances the Apache's fearsome reputation with a claimed 400 percent increase in target destruction and a 720 percent increase in survivability. All the existing AH-64A variants of the Apache are to be upgraded to AH-64D Longbow standards.

SPECIFICATIONS

Manufacturer:	*The Boeing Company*
Mission:	*multi-mission attack*
Length:	*17.7m (58ft)*
Height:	*4m (13ft)*
Rotor Diameter:	*14.6 (48ft)*
Crew:	*2*
Propulsion:	*2 x GE T700-701C*
Horsepower:	*1940 shaft horsepower*
Maximum Speed:	*365km/h (227mph)*
Cruise Speed:	*265km/h (165mph)*
Vertical Rate of Climb:	*450m/min (1475ft/min)*
Range:	*407km (253 miles)*
Weight:	*7800kg (17,000lb)*
Date Deployed:	*1998*
Guns:	*1 x M230 30mm chain gun*
Missiles:	*FFAR, Hellfire, Sidearm, AIM-9*
Systems:	*TADS/PNVG, Longbow radar*

BA609

A trial of the BA609 tilt-rotor aircraft is currently taking place with the United States Coast Guard (USCG), leading to a possible introduction into the existing helicopter fleet as a potential replacement for established aircraft types. The BA609 uses the same type of technology employed on the V-22 Osprey. In fact, much of the research and development that went into the Osprey was evaluated during the creation of the BA609, but it is a completely new design. As aviation companies look to expand their customer bases beyond that of either purely the military or commercial businesses, the BA609 is an aircraft that can cross the boundaries. Thus the USCG has the aircraft on trial, while other military organizations around the world have placed small orders to test and evaluate the tilt-rotor concept. The advantages of an aircraft that can take off or land vertically, and then utilize the straight-line speed of a fixed-wing aircraft, are obvious, and already demonstrated by the successful Harrier jet fighter-bomber. However, it is only with technological developments in recent years that a tilt-rotor aircraft has become a viable proposition. Should the trials of the BA609 prove successful, then it will not only be an excellent addition to the USCG fleet but will probably find other military applications.

SPECIFICATIONS

Manufacturer:	*Agusta/Bell Helicopter Textron*
Mission:	*SAR*
Length:	*13.3m (44ft)*
Height:	*4.5m (15ft)*
Rotor Diameter:	*2 x 7.9m (26ft)*
Crew:	*2*
Propulsion:	*2 x P & W Canada PT6C*
Horsepower:	*3800 shaft horsepower*
Maximum Speed:	*510km/h (318mph)*
Cruise Speed:	*465km/h (290mph)*
Vertical Rate of Climb:	*not available*
Range:	*1500km (937 miles)*
Weight:	*4765kg (10,483lb)*
Date Deployed:	*2002*
Guns:	*none*
Missiles:	*none*
Systems:	*GPS*

CH-46E SEA KNIGHT

The CH-46E Sea Knight is an ageing yet integral part of the USMC assault forces. Troop assault is the primary function of this distinctive twin-rotor helicopter, and the movement of supplies and equipment is secondary. Additional tasks can be combat and assault support for evacuation and other maritime special operations, over-water SAR augmentation, support for mobile forward refuelling and re-arming points or aeromedical evacuation of casualties from the field to suitable medical facilities. The CH-46 Sea Knight was first procured in 1964 to meet the medium-lift requirements of the USMC in Vietnam, but its transition from the design phase to operations was far from smooth. A great many aircraft were lost during development, and troops were initially sceptical about it. However, it quickly won over its doubters and has served with great success in all combat and peacetime environments. It is nearing the end of its operational life, as normal airframe operational and attrition rates have taken the aircraft to the point where a medium-lift replacement is required. The V-22 Osprey has been designated as its replacement, and there is a certain irony in the fact that the USMC is as sceptical about the new aircraft as it was 40 years ago about the Sea Knight.

SPECIFICATIONS

Manufacturer:	*The Boeing Company*
Mission:	*medium-lift assault*
Length:	*13.9m (45ft)*
Height:	*5m (16ft)*
Rotor Diameter:	*2 x 15.2m (50ft)*
Crew:	*4*
Propulsion:	*2 x GE T58*
Horsepower:	*3600 shaft horsepower*
Maximum Speed:	*267km/h (166mph)*
Cruise Speed:	*222km/h (138mph)*
Vertical Rate of Climb:	*522m/min (1715ft/min)*
Range:	*1111km (690 miles)*
Weight:	*7257kg (16,000lb)*
Date Deployed:	*1978*
Guns:	*2 x 7.62mm M-60 machine guns*
Missiles:	*none*
Systems:	*PNVG*

CH-47D CHINOOK

The CH-47 Chinook is a tandem-rotored, twin-engined, medium-lift helicopter. It has a crew of four, comprising a pilot, a navigator and two crewmen. It is capable of carrying 45 fully equipped troops or a variety of heavy loads up to approximately 10.1 tonnes (10 tons). It is a rugged and reliable aircraft, and has been at the forefront of US military operations for several decades. It is in service with a number of armed forces around the world, including Britain. During the Falklands War it is reported that, at one stage, 80 fully equipped troops were carried in one lift by an RAF Chinook. Indeed, during a Gulf War mission, a single US Chinook carried 110 Iraqi prisoners of war. The Chinook has a famous load-carrying capability, able to transport a wide range of equipment. Its primary mission is moving artillery, ammunition, personnel and supplies, but it also performs rescue, aeromedical, parachuting, aircraft recovery and special operations missions. The image of a Chinook with an artillery piece or jeep underslung is one of the most iconic in modern warfare. Despite the age of the design, the Chinook has many years left in it. The first-rate military powers have recently finished updating their Chinooks to the newest CH-47D model, and the US will be upgrading once more to the Improved Cargo Helicopter (ICH) model by 2004.

SPECIFICATIONS

Manufacturer:	*The Boeing Company*
Mission:	*medium support*
Length:	*15.5m (51ft)*
Height:	*5.7m (19ft)*
Rotor Diameter:	*2 x 18.3m (60ft)*
Crew:	*4*
Propulsion:	*2 x Textron Lycoming T55-L-712*
Horsepower:	*7500 shaft horsepower*
Maximum Speed:	*269km/h (167mph)*
Cruise Speed:	*265km/h (165mph)*
Vertical Rate of Climb:	*561m/min (1841ft/min)*
Range:	*600km (375 miles)*
Weight:	*10,814kg (23,790lb)*
Date Deployed:	*1987*
Guns:	*3 x 7.62mm M-60 machine guns*
Missiles:	*none*
Systems:	*GPS, PNVG*

CH-53E SEA STALLION

Sea Stallions are the US Navy's heavy-lift helicopters, capable of carrying up to 16,330kg (36,000lb), including artillery pieces and light armour. The machines can also retrieve downed aircraft, including another CH-53E. This massive lifting power has proved invaluable to the US Navy since the aircraft entered service in the early 1980s. Derived from the 1960s vintage CH-53 family, the CH-53E incorporates a third engine to give it extra lifting power. It is now the standard heavy lift helicopter for the USMC. Its size generally restricts it to operations from amphibious landing craft and aircraft carriers but, since these ships form the backbone of any amphibious assault, there is no need for deployment aboard other ships. In addition to its lifting power, the CH-53E can be refuelled while in flight, giving it a much increased range. In 1990, two CH-53E Sea Stallions flew 856km (532 miles), refuelling mid-flight twice, to rescue US and foreign allies from the US Embassy in Mogadishu, Somalia. They saw further action in Bosnia, where two CH-53Es rescued downed US pilot Captain Scott O'Grady in 1995. The CH-53E is due to remain in service until the V-22 Osprey replaces it, and thus is undergoing a programme of upgrades and improvements to keep it airworthy until 2015.

SPECIFICATIONS

Manufacturer:	*Sikorsky Aircraft*
Mission:	*ship-based heavy-lift*
Length:	*30m (99ft)*
Height:	*8.5m (28ft)*
Rotor Diameter:	*24m (79ft)*
Crew:	*3/4*
Propulsion:	*3 x GE T64-416*
Horsepower:	*13,500 shaft horsepower*
Maximum Speed:	*315km/h (195mph)*
Cruise Speed:	*278km/h (172mph)*
Vertical Rate of Climb:	*750m/min (2500ft/min)*
Range:	*889km (550 miles)*
Weight:	*15,102kg (33,226lb)*
Date Deployed:	*1981*
Guns:	*2 x .50in machine guns*
Missiles:	*Sidewinder*
Systems:	*GPS, FLIR, chaff and flare dispenser*

CH-54A TARHE

The Sikorsky CH-54A Tarhe or Skycrane, with a crew of three, was designed for heavy internal or external lift of large bulk loads. It has a rear-facing pilot's seat to provide a clear view of the cargo. A hoist allows for the pickup and delivery of cargo without the need to land. One of the most interesting features of this helicopter, and most unusual in the world of aviation, is the utility of a vehicle stowed in the cargo area. A lightweight van (universal pod) could be attached to the fuselage for use as a mobile command post, maintenance and repair shop, or as a Mobile Army Surgical Hospital (MASH). Thus the Tarhe could be used as a rapid reaction mobile field hospital, able to medevac serious casualties, having given them first aid on the ground. A people pod was also designed to carry 45 combat-ready troops, and the Skycrane served with the 1st Cavalry Division in Vietnam. It was used in aircraft recovery operations when loads were too heavy for the CH-47 Chinook. It was also useful for offloading during ship-to-shore operations. On occasion the CH-54 could also be rigged to drop the 4536kg (10,000lb) daisy-cutter cratering bomb used to create landing zones in dense jungle. It was a truly useful helicopter, but was replaced by the less powerful but more flexible CH-47 Chinook. It now serves only in the US Army reserve forces.

SPECIFICATIONS

Manufacturer:	Sikorsky Aircraft
Mission:	heavy-lift transport
Length:	26.9m (88ft)
Height:	5.6m (19ft)
Rotor Diameter:	21.9m (72ft)
Crew:	3
Propulsion:	2 x Pratt & Whitney JFTD12-5A
Horsepower:	9350 shaft horsepower
Maximum Speed:	202km/h (126mph)
Cruise Speed:	169km/h (105mph)
Vertical Rate of Climb:	405m/min (1330ft/min)
Range:	370km (230 miles)
Weight:	8722kg (19,234lb)
Date Deployed:	1964
Guns:	none
Missiles:	none
Systems:	hoist, universal pod

SH-3 SEA KING

One of the world's most familiar helicopters, the SH-3 Sea King is a twin-engine, all-weather aircraft. The turbine-engined Sikorsky S-61 spawned a family of submarine hunters, airliners and rescue helicopters with offspring still serving around the world. Born as the Sea King anti-submarine helicopter for the US Navy, originally named HSS-2, the S-61 grew into different models and is now used by several countries. Although designed as an anti-submarine helicopter, it has been replaced in this role by newer, more capable aircraft. However, its utility has meant that it continues to serve in forces around the world, in some cases continuing in its original role as an ASW helicopter, but in most cases remodelled as a logistics or SAR aircraft. One of its most interesting design aspects is the boat-type hull, which allows it to remain bouyant for a time if forced to ditch into water. The basic H-3 design can easily be outfitted to perform many different roles, and it is this flexibility, along with its all-round ability, that has made it popular across the globe. The US and other technologically advanced countries have begun to replace the Sea King. However, the unhurried nature of defence development, procurement and delivery means that the helicopters will remain a familiar sight for many years to come.

SPECIFICATIONS

Manufacturer:	Sikorsky Aircraft
Mission:	logistical support
Length:	21.9m (73ft)
Height:	5.1m (17ft)
Rotor Diameter:	18.9m (62ft)
Crew:	4
Propulsion:	2 x GE T58-8F
Horsepower:	2850 shaft horsepower
Maximum Speed:	267km/h (166mph)
Cruise Speed:	217km/h (138mph)
Vertical Rate of Climb:	409m/min (1350ft/min)
Range:	1006km (625 miles)
Weight:	5339kg (11,865lb)
Date Deployed:	1961
Guns:	none
Missiles:	none
Systems:	GPS

HH-3E

Sikorsky's Jolly Green Giant, or HH-3E, is a heavy-lift helicopter employed by the US Army. It is used for recovery of personnel and aerospace hardware in support of global air and space operations. The twin-engined aircraft has also been used for combat and special operations. A modified version of the CH-3 transport helicopter, the HH-3E was developed for aircrew rescue missions deep in enemy-held territory during the Vietnam War. Many downed aircrews were rescued by Jolly Green Giants and their crews. This long-range machine has a hydraulically operated rear ramp for straight-inloading, and an ejectable sliding door on the right side at the front of the cabin. It has built-in equipment for the removal and replacement of all major components in remote areas. The Jolly Green Giant has an automatic flight-control system, instrumentation for all-weather operation, and Doppler navigation equipment. The HH-3E made the record books by making the first non-stop transatlantic flight by a helicopter in 1967, when two aircraft flew from New York City to the Paris air show. During that 6832km (4270-mile) flight, which took 30 hours and 46 minutes, each aircraft was aerially refueled nine times. The Jolly Green Giant has also seen more recent action, flying 251 combat missions during Operation Desert Storm in 1991.

SPECIFICATIONS

Manufacturer:	*Sikorsky Aircraft*
Mission:	*combat recovery, special ops*
Length:	*22m (73ft)*
Height:	*5.5m (18ft)*
Rotor Diameter:	*18.8m (62ft)*
Crew:	*4*
Propulsion:	*2 x GE T58-5*
Horsepower:	*2900 shaft horsepower*
Maximum Speed:	*265km/h (165mph)*
Cruise Speed:	*243km/h (151mph)*
Vertical Rate of Climb:	*506m/min (1660ft/min)*
Range:	*965km (600 miles)*
Weight:	*5635kg (12,423lb)*
Date Deployed:	*1966*
Guns:	*none*
Missiles:	*none*
Systems:	*Doppler navigation equipment*

HH-60J JAYHAWK

The HH-60J Jayhawk is a medium-range recovery helicopter. It is used to perform SAR, law enforcement, military readiness and marine environmental protection missions. The USCG added 42 Jayhawks to its fleet of aircraft, replacing the Sikorsky HH-3F Pelican helicopters that the Coastguard has used for more than 20 years. The HH-60J is similar to the HH-3F in many ways, and the assigned missions are the same. However, the HH-60J has numerous upgrades including a state-of-the-art electronics package. The HH-60J is lighter, faster and the engines have more power. The Jayhawk can fly 480km (300 miles) offshore, remain on-scene for 45 minutes, recover six survivors, and return with spare fuel in reserve. The Jayhawk's cutting-edge radar, radio and navigation equipment enables the helicopter to carry out the USCG's SAR, law enforcement, military readiness and marine environmental protection missions efficiently and effectively. The Jayhawk uses the NAVSTAR Global Positioning System (GPS) as its primary long-range navigational aid. On board the Jayhawk, the Collins RCVR-3A radio simultaneously receives information from four of the system's 18 worldwide satellites and converts it into latitude fixes, pinpointing the helicopter's position.

SPECIFICATIONS

Manufacturer:	Sikorsky Aircraft
Mission:	SAR
Length:	13.6m (45ft)
Height:	5m (17ft)
Rotor Diameter:	16.4m (54ft)
Crew:	4
Propulsion:	2 x GE T700-401C
Horsepower:	3750 shaft horsepower
Maximum Speed:	333km/h (207mph)
Cruise Speed:	259km/h (161mph)
Vertical Rate of Climb:	not available
Range:	1296km (805 miles)
Weight:	6590kg (14,500lb)
Date Deployed:	1991
Guns:	none
Missiles:	none
Systems:	GPS, winch, Collins RCVR radio

HH-65A DOLPHIN

The USCG has added 96 short-range HH-65A helicopters to its fleet to replace the HH-52A Sikorsky Sea Guard. Although normally stationed onshore, the Dolphins can be carried on board medium- and high-endurance Coast Guard Cutters. They assist in the missions of SAR, law enforcement (including drug interdiction), polar ice-breaking, marine environmental protection (including pollution control) and military readiness. Helicopters stationed aboard icebreakers are the ships' eyes to find more navigable ice channels. They also airlift supplies to ships and to villages isolated by adverse weather. HH-65As are made of corrosion-resistant, composite materials. The shrouded tail rotor is unique to the Dolphin. Another special feature is its computerized flight management system that integrates state-of-the-art communications and navigation equipment. This system provides automatic flight control. At the pilot's direction, the system will bring the aircraft to a stable hover 15m (50ft) above a selected object. This is an important safety feature in darkness or in hazardous weather, which is quite common in USCG operations. The computer can select search patterns that can be flown automatically, freeing the pilot and co-pilot to concentrate on locating the object of the search.

SPECIFICATIONS

Manufacturer:	Aerospatiale/Textron Lycoming
Mission:	SAR, law enforcement
Length:	13.3m (44ft)
Height:	3.9m (13ft)
Rotor Diameter:	11.8m (39ft)
Crew:	4
Propulsion:	2 x Lycoming LTS
Horsepower:	1350 shaft horsepower
Maximum Speed:	296km/h (184mph)
Cruise Speed:	222km/h (138mph)
Vertical Rate of Climb:	not available
Range:	565km (353 miles)
Weight:	2750kg (6052lb)
Date Deployed:	1983
Guns:	none
Missiles:	none
Systems:	computerized flight system, GPS

K-1200 KMAX

Kaman's K-1200 KMAX helicopter is a unique design in the world of aviation. The main principle behind it is Kaman's intermeshing rotor technology with servo-flap control, which is exceptionally efficient at lifting heavy loads. The aircraft has counter-rotating main rotors and no tail rotor, which means all engine power goes directly to the main rotors for the highest lifting capacity of any rotor configuration. The aircraft's rugged construction allows it to fly repetitive, short operational cycles eight to 10 hours a day. This has interested a number of parties, which are keen to utilize the KMAX's lifting power. These potential purchasers range from lumber companies to oil firms and, of course, the military. The KMAX has demonstrated successfully its capability to perform vertical supply replenishment of US Navy ships at sea. However, the USMC envisages a pilotless KMAX fulfilling a new tactical concept for re-supplying troops on land from fast-moving ships at sea. The future of the KMAX is clearly unmanned. Yet, until this becomes a viable option, the KMAX will continue to be flown by one pilot. When the technology becomes viable for the KMAX to be fully automated, it could herald a revolution in the way in which the USMC conducts its operations.

SPECIFICATIONS

Manufacturer:	*Kaman Aerospace*
Mission:	*external-lift transport*
Length:	*15.9m (52ft)*
Height:	*4.1m (13ft)*
Rotor Diameter:	*2x 14.7m (48ft)*
Crew:	*1*
Propulsion:	*1 x Allied Signal T-5317A-1*
Horsepower:	*1500 shaft horsepower*
Maximum Speed:	*185km/h (115mph)*
Cruise Speed:	*165km/h (102mph)*
Vertical Rate of Climb:	*762m/min (2500ft/min)*
Range:	*460km (285 miles)*
Weight:	*2313kg (5100lb)*
Date Deployed:	*1994*
Guns:	*none*
Missiles:	*none*
Systems:	*not available*

MH-47E SOA CHINOOK

The MH-47E Special Operations Aircraft (SOA) is a derivative of the Boeing CH-47 Chinook. Included with other adaptations is a significantly increased fuel capacity with modified main and auxiliary fuel tanks. The aircraft's integrated avionics suites and multi-mode radars have also been updated. It is intended to provide adverse-weather infiltration/extraction and support to US armed forces, country teams, other agencies and special activities. The CH-47D Chinook has been specially modified to perform special operations missions, and has been tested in combat. It provides long-range penetration, medium-assault helicopter support to special operations. During Operation Desert Storm in 1991, the MH-47E's predecessor, the CH-47, conducted infiltration and extraction of special forces troops and downed pilots. The distinctive twin-rotor design of the MH-47E makes it one of the most easily recognizable helicopters in the world. In the case of the special forces Chinook it is also one of the most technologically advanced. Capable of flying low level over any terrain, in any conditions, the MH-47E has become a firm favourite with special forces the world over, and is used extensively by the US Delta Force and the British SAS. The Chinook is equipped with a suite of countermeasure systems selected by the customer country.

SPECIFICATIONS

Manufacturer:	*The Boeing Company*
Mission:	*covert infiltration of special forces*
Length:	*15.6m (51ft)*
Height:	*5.8m (19ft)*
Rotor Diameter:	*2 x 18.3m (60ft)*
Crew:	*3*
Propulsion:	*2 x Textron Lycoming T55-L-712*
Horsepower:	*7500 shaft horsepower*
Maximum Speed:	*269km/h (167mph)*
Cruise Speed:	*265km/h (165mph)*
Vertical Rate of Climb:	*561m/min (1841ft/min)*
Range:	*1136km (705 miles)*
Weight:	*12,210kg (27,000lb)*
Date Deployed:	*1993*
Guns:	*6 x M-60 machine guns*
Missiles:	*none*
Systems:	*FLIR, terrain radar, flare/chaff*

MH-53J PAVE LOW III

Low-level, long-range, undetected penetration into denied areas, day or night, in adverse weather conditions is the mission of the MH-53J Pave Low IIIE helicopter. It specializes in the infiltration, extraction and re-supply of special operations forces. The Pave Low III heavy-lift helicopter is one of the largest and most powerful in the US Air Force (USAF) inventory, and one of the most technologically advanced helicopters in the world. Its terrain-following, terrain-avoidance radar and FLIR sensor, along with a projected map display, enable the crew to follow terrain contours and avoid obstacles, making low-level penetration possible. The helicopter is equipped with armour plating, and a combination of three 7.62mm miniguns or .50-calibre machine guns. It can transport 38 troops and has an external cargo hook with a 9000kg (20,000lb) capacity. Derived from the Sikorsky HH-3E Jolly Green Giant, its modifications include the aforementioned FLIR, GPS, Doppler navigation systems, an on-board computer and integrated avionics to enable precise navigation to and from target areas. The MH-53J Pave Low saw extensive action during Operation Desert Storm, and has been in continual use as a special operations infiltration/extraction helicopter.

SPECIFICATIONS

Manufacturer:	*Sikorsky Aircraft*
Mission:	*covert infiltration/extraction*
Length:	*28m (92ft)*
Height:	*7.6m (25ft)*
Rotor Diameter:	*21.9m (72ft)*
Crew:	*6*
Propulsion:	*2 x GE T64-416*
Horsepower:	*8500 shaft horsepower*
Maximum Speed:	*320km/h (199mph)*
Cruise Speed:	*264km/h (165mph)*
Vertical Rate of Climb:	*762m/min (2500ft/min)*
Range:	*1014km (630 miles)*
Weight:	*16,561kg (36,435lb)*
Date Deployed:	*1981*
Guns:	*3 x 7.62mm miniguns*
Missiles:	*none*
Systems:	*GPS, FLIR, terrain-following radar*

MH-60G PAVE HAWK

The MH-60G Pave Hawk is a modern, medium-lift, special operations helicopter for missions requiring medium- to long-range infiltration, extraction and re-supply of special operations forces on land or sea. It is equipped with FLIR to enable its crew to follow more easily terrain contours and avoid obstacles at night. The MH-60G's primary wartime missions are special operations forces support in day, night or marginal weather conditions. Other missions include combat SAR. As a highly modified variant of the UH-60A Black Hawk, the MH-60G offers increased capability in range (endurance), navigation, communications and defensive systems. It can be used to provide a full range of special air warfare activities including special operations, psychological operations and civil affairs. The MH-60G can be deployed by airlift or sealift, and it can also be self-deployed. The preferred option is airlift using a C-5 Galaxy fixed-wing aircraft, and is essential if rapid deployment is required. A Galaxy can transport a maximum of five MH-60Gs. The aircraft can be broken down for shipment in less than one hour and off-loaded and rebuilt at the location in less than two hours. The optimum deployment package is four MH-60Gs via a C-5.

SPECIFICATIONS

Manufacturer:	*Sikorsky Aircraft*
Mission:	*special operations*
Length:	*13.6m (45ft)*
Height:	*5m (17ft)*
Rotor Diameter:	*16.4m (54ft)*
Crew:	*4*
Propulsion:	*2 x GE T700-701C*
Horsepower:	*3000 shaft horsepower*
Maximum Speed:	*294km/h (184mph)*
Cruise Speed:	*270km/h (171mph)*
Vertical Rate of Climb:	*not available*
Range:	*833km (517 miles)*
Weight:	*6590kg (14,500lb)*
Date Deployed:	*1994*
Guns:	*1 x 7.62mm M-60 machine gun*
Missiles:	*none*
Systems:	*GPS, PNVG, terrain-following radar*

MH-68A ENFORCER

A specially built version of the commercial Agusta A109 Power, the MH-68A Enforcer is in service with the USCG. It made its first operational flight in 2000. The Coastguard has recently deployed a number of these aircraft to be used primarily in its anti-drug operations. They operate from the flight-deck of the USCG's medium-endurance cutters as part of its counter-narcotics mission. It has become necessary for USCG helicopters to be armed because of the increased sophistication of the drug cartels, not to mention their increased willingness to take on US ships and aircraft. The MH-68 is a particularly well-equipped machine, with a rescue hoist, emergency floats, .50-calibre sniper rifle with laser sight, M-240 machine gun, PNVG, FLIR, Light Eye and NightSun searchlight. Avionics include a fully integrated avionics suite, Head-Up Display (HUD) and GPS moving map. It has already seen a great deal of action and scored a remarkable number of successes. Use of the helicopter by the USCG allows the Coastuard to bring down precise fire on to the target vessel in order to disable it. This strategy has contributed greatly to the improvement in the USCG's anti-drugs success rate.

SPECIFICATIONS

Manufacturer:	Agusta
Mission:	coast guard, law enforcement
Length:	13.5m (43ft)
Height:	3.3m (10ft)
Rotor Diameter:	11m (36ft)
Crew:	3
Propulsion:	2 x P & W Canada PW206C
Horsepower:	800 shaft horsepower
Maximum Speed:	305km/h (190mph)
Cruise Speed:	265km/h (165mph)
Vertical Rate of Climb:	not available
Range:	565km (353 miles)
Weight:	1415kg (3113lb)
Date Deployed:	2000
Guns:	1 x .50in rifle, M-240 machine gun
Missiles:	none
Systems:	GPS, FLIR, PNVG, searchlight, hoist

OH-58D KIOWA

Bell's OH-58D Kiowa Warrior is an aircraft that was born not from conceptual ideas but from the need to counter the threat posed by gunboats to vital shipping in the Persian Gulf during 1987. Developed from the successful OH-58 series of light helicopters, the Kiowa Warrior is an armed reconnaissance aircraft carrying a crew of two. It was conceived and developed in less than 100 days and was so successful in deterring gunboat activity that the US Army was immediately convinced of its capabilities and placed an order for all existing OH-58 Kiowas to be upgraded. The current version will eventually be replaced by the Comanche, but until then the OH-58D is a vital component of the US Army's aerial fighting force. The machine is equipped with one .50in heavy machine gun and can carry FFAR rockets, Stinger and Hellfire missiles. The primary mission of the Kiowa Warrior is armed reconnaissance in air cavalry and light attack companies. In addition, the Kiowa Warrior may be called upon to participate in other missions or tasks such as joint air attack operations, air combat, limited attack operation or artillery target designation. The distinctive mast-mounted sight, which incorporates a thermal imaging system, a laser range finder, a television sensor and a boresight system, is one of the key elements of the Kiowa Warrior.

SPECIFICATIONS

Manufacturer:	*Bell Helicopter Textron*
Mission:	*armed reconnaissance*
Length:	*12.5m (41ft)*
Height:	*4m (13ft)*
Rotor Diameter:	*10.7m (35ft)*
Crew:	*2*
Propulsion:	*1 x T703-AD-700*
Horsepower:	*650 shaft horsepower*
Maximum Speed:	*237km/h (147mph)*
Cruise Speed:	*166km/h (100mph)*
Vertical Rate of Climb:	*152m/min (500ft/min)*
Range:	*480km (300 miles)*
Weight:	*2040kg (4500lb)*
Date Deployed:	*1991*
Guns:	*1 x 50in heavy machine gun*
Missiles:	*FFAR, Stinger, Hellfire*
Systems:	*thermal imaging, rangefinder*

OH-6A CAYUSE

The Boeing OH-6A was designed for use as a military scout during the Vietnam War to meet the US Army's need for an extremely manoeuvrable light-observation helicopter. The Hughes OH-6A Cayuse was quite effective when teamed with the AH-1G Cobra attack helicopter. The OH-6A Loach would find targets by flying low, "trolling" for fire, and lead in a Cobra, or Snake, to attack. The OH-6A can be armed with the M-27 armament subsystem, the M-134 six-barrel 7.62mm "minigun" or the M-129 40mm grenade launcher on the XM8 armament subsystem. Two special operations versions of the OH-6A are the Little Bird AH-6C armed variant, and the MH-6B transport/utility version, which can carry up to six personnel for quick insertion and extraction missions. A previous version, the EH-6B, was used for command, control and radio relay. The MH-6 Little Bird is the only light-assault helicopter in the army inventory. It provides assault-helicopter support to special operations forces, and can be armed with a combination of guns and FFAR. It has an un-refuelled range of 463km (250 nautical miles). The AH-6 Little Bird Gun, a light-attack version of the helicopter, has been tested and proven in combat when armed with guns, Hellfire missiles and 2.75in FFAR rockets.

SPECIFICATIONS

Manufacturer:	The Boeing Company
Mission:	armed reconnaissance
Length:	7.6m (25ft)
Height:	2.6m (8ft)
Rotor Diameter:	8m (26ft)
Crew:	2
Propulsion:	1 x Allison T63
Horsepower:	317 shaft horsepower
Maximum Speed:	241km/h (149mph)
Cruise Speed:	221km/h (137mph)
Vertical Rate of Climb:	504m/min (1654ft/min)
Range:	485km (301 miles)
Weight:	896kg (1975lb)
Date Deployed:	1962
Guns:	1 x 7.62mm machine gun
Missiles:	grenade launcher, FFAR
Systems:	GPS, FLIR. chaff/flare dispenser

RAH-66 COMANCHE

The RAH-66 Comanche is believed to represent the future of the US aerial reconnaissance and light attack helicopter force, and is expected to be a key element in the strategic vision of achieving dominant battlespace awareness. Its primary role will be to seek out enemy forces and designate targets for the AH-64 Apache attack helicopter. This can take place at night, in adverse weather and on obscured battlefields, using advanced infrared sensors. To succeed in this role, the Comanche has been designed with speed and stealth in mind. Coupled with the next generation of sophisticated sensors and weapons systems, this makes it a truly formidable aircraft. The Comanche incorporates more low-observable stealth features than any aircraft in US Army history, with the radar cross-section (RCS) being less than that of a Hellfire missile. To reduce RCS, weapons can be carried internally, the gun can be rotated aft and stowed within a fairing behind the turret when not in use, and the landing gear is fully retractable. In short, the Comanche has no peers. Military budgets permitting, when it is officially brought into service in 2006, the US Army will have at its disposal a vastly capable, sophisticated and versatile helicopter to provide unparalleled target detection and acquisition.

SPECIFICATIONS

Manufacturer:	*Boeing Sikorsky*
Mission:	*reconnaissance, attack*
Length:	*12.7m (42ft)*
Height:	*3.3m (11ft)*
Rotor Diameter:	*11.8m (39ft)*
Crew:	*2*
Propulsion:	*2 x T800-LHTEC-801*
Horsepower:	*3126 shaft horsepower*
Maximum Speed:	*330 km/h (206mph)*
Cruise Speed:	*310 km/h (193mph)*
Vertical Rate of Climb:	*530m/min (1750ft/min)*
Range:	*480km (300 miles)*
Weight:	*3950kg (8690lb)*
Date Deployed:	*2006*
Guns:	*1 x XM301 20mm auto-cannon*
Missiles:	*Hellfire, Stinger, 70mm FFAR*
Systems:	*GPS, FLIR*

S-92 HELIBUS

Sikorsky's S-92 Helibus is based on the proven US Army UH-60 Black Hawk and US Navy SH-60 Seahawk helicopters. The manufacturer is actively marketing the S-92 for military requirements in Canada, Portugal and Scandinavia. The Helibus is designed to answer the needs of users requiring greater payload and range characteristics than those provided by the Black Hawk. Improvements include more powerful engines, seating capacity for 22 troops in the stretched cabin, and a rear loading ramp. It has been designed to compete directly against Europe's EH 101 Merlin, the NH-90 and a variety of Eurocopter-built medium-utility aircraft. The S-92 is a truly multinational effort, with manufacturers from many countries contributing to the project. These include Mitsubishi Heavy Industries of Japan (main cabin), Jingdezhen Helicopter Group of China (vertical tail surfaces), Gamesa of Spain (aft transmission tailcone and "strongback" composite structure), Aerospace Industrial Development Corporation of Taiwan (flight deck and other parts) and Embraer of Brazil (sponsons, fuel cells and gauging systems). Despite an initial lack of firm orders, Sikorsky remains confident that the S-92 will be drafted into service with a number of armed forces to replace their current fleets.

SPECIFICATIONS

Manufacturer:	*Sikorsky Aircraft*
Mission:	*medium utility*
Length:	*17.3m (57ft)*
Height:	*6.4m (21ft)*
Rotor Diameter:	*17.7m (58ft)*
Crew:	*3*
Propulsion:	*2 x CT7-8*
Horsepower:	*4800 shaft horsepower*
Maximum Speed:	*280km/h (175mph)*
Cruise Speed:	*252km/h (157mph)*
Vertical Rate of Climb:	*not available*
Range:	*880km (550 miles)*
Weight:	*7030kg (15,500lb)*
Date Deployed:	*2001*
Guns:	*2 x 7.62mm machine guns*
Missiles:	*none*
Systems:	*GPS, PNVG*

SH-60B SEAHAWK

The Sikorsky-built SH-60B Seahawk is the US Navy version of the US Army's highly effective UH-60 Black Hawk helicopter. It can fulfil many different roles, ranging from ASW, medevac and SAR. However, this particular aircraft is used primarily as an ASW platform, based onboard US Navy frigates, destroyers and cruisers. Introduced during the 1980s, the SH-60 Seahawk has become the standard aircraft onboard a great many of the US Navy's warships and has seen service throughout the world. Designed and built during the height of the Cold War with the former USSR, it was originally tasked to hunt Soviet submarines, although its original remit has now been expanded to take on other roles. The Seahawk, with its crew of three, can lower its sonobuoy, acoustic equipment or MAD more than 450m (1500ft) into the ocean and then detect or track enemy submarines. If configured to do so, the SH-60 can use Mk 50 torpedoes to attack any targets to a range of around 1500m (5000ft). In addition to its own armament and systems, the SH-60 has a datalink connected to its parent ship through which it can send and receive information on targets in the area of operation. It can thereby increase greatly the efficiency of the US Navy's various fleets in locating and neutralizing any subsea threats.

SPECIFICATIONS

Manufacturer:	Sikorsky Aircraft
Mission:	ASW
Length:	15.3m (50ft)
Height:	3.8m (13ft)
Rotor Diameter:	16.4m (54ft)
Crew:	3
Propulsion:	2 x GE T700-701C
Horsepower:	3400 shaft horsepower
Maximum Speed:	296km/h (184mph)
Cruise Speed:	250km/h (155mph)
Vertical Rate of Climb:	545m/min (1800ft/min)
Range:	833km (518 miles)
Weight:	6191kg (13,650lb)
Date Deployed:	1983
Guns:	1 x 7.62mm M-60 machine gun
Missiles:	Mk 50 torpedoes, Penguin AGM
Systems:	GPS, LAMPS, RAST, sonobuoy

TH-67 CREEK

Bell Helicopter Textron has built the US Army's TH-67 New Training Helicopter (NTH), developed from the hugely successful Bell 206 JetRanger. The aircraft's function is to replace existing UH-1H Hueys being used to train Initial Entry Rotary Wing (IERW) students. These Hueys have been the army's interim trainer since the 1988 retirement of the TH-55 Osage. The TH-67 Creek is a state-of-the-art helicopter and the aircraft of choice for a new generation of army aviators. In the tactical portion of pilot training, the OH-58 Kiowa is still the helicopter used given its war-configured characteristics. But, for IERW flight instruction, the new TH-67 is the ideal machine. For a new Aviation Lieutenant, flight school means the successful completion of Aviation Officer Basic Course (AVOBC) Phase I, AVOBC Phase II IERW Qualification, AVOBC Phase III, and an Advanced Aircraft Qualification Course (AAQC). Every two weeks, an IERW class starts and the TH-67 Creek's primary mission begins. The first 20 weeks of training involve learning the basics of helicopter flight and instruments in the TH-67. At the end of primary flight and instruments, most officers will move on to Basic Combat Skills (BCS) and PNVG in the Bell-designed OH-58C Kiowa.

SPECIFICATIONS

Manufacturer:	*Bell Helicopter Textron*
Mission:	*training*
Length:	*9.5m (31ft)*
Height:	*2.9m (10ft)*
Rotor Diameter:	*10.2m (34ft)*
Crew:	*1*
Propulsion:	*1 x Alison 250-C20J*
Horsepower:	*420 shaft horsepower*
Maximum Speed:	*225km/h (140mph)*
Cruise Speed:	*216km/h (135mph)*
Vertical Rate of Climb:	*384m/min (1267ft/min)*
Range:	*748km (467 miles)*
Weight:	*742kg (1632lb)*
Date Deployed:	*2001*
Guns:	*none*
Missiles:	*none*
Systems:	*basic flight systems*

UH-1H HUEY

legend, the remarkable Bell UH-1 Iroquois (Huey) is the most famous helicopter in the world, linked forever with images of the Vietnam War. It has been the quintessential all-purpose military helicopter for more than three decades. It has been used by all four US services and international forces in missions ranging from mountain rescue to troop transport, and from anti-armour to ASW. The Huey got its distinctive nickname from its original US Army designation, the HU-1. It was later redesignated UH-1, under a tri-service agreement. The UH-1 Iroquois is used for command and control, medical evacuation, and to transport personnel, equipment and supplies. The latest models are the UH-1H and the UH-1V. Initially procured in 1959, the Huey is the senior member of the army's helicopter fleet. The last production aircraft was delivered in 1976. More than 9000 were produced in 20 years, evolving through 13 models. Considered to be the most widely used helicopter in the world, the Huey is flown by about 40 countries. In 1995 the army's UH-1 residual fleet was projected to be approximately 1000 aircraft. Though the technology in the UH-1 has been largely made redundant by newer aircraft, the US armed forces still envisage keeping 700 aircraft in service until 2015.

SPECIFICATIONS

Manufacturer:	*Bell Helicopter Textron*
Mission:	*multi-role transport*
Length:	*12.8m (42ft)*
Height:	*4.4m (14ft)*
Rotor Diameter:	*14.6m (48ft)*
Crew:	*3*
Propulsion:	*1 x Lycoming T53-L13B*
Horsepower:	*1100 shaft horsepower*
Maximum Speed:	*204km/h (127mph)*
Cruise Speed:	*185km/h (115mph)*
Vertical Rate of Climb:	*485m/min (1600ft/min)*
Range:	*370km (231 miles)*
Weight:	*2600kg (5800lb)*
Date Deployed:	*1985*
Guns:	*2 x 7.62mm M-60 machine guns*
Missiles:	*none*
Systems:	*PNVG, rescue winch, searchlight*

UH-1N HUEY

One successful variant of the renowned Huey is the UH-1N light-lift utility helicopter, used by the US Air Force Space Command (USAFSC) missile wings and groups. Its primary roles include airlift of emergency security and disaster response forces, security surveillance of off-base nuclear weapons movements, space shuttle landing support and SAR operations. The USMC and US Army both use the UH-1N because of the speed with which it can be reconfigured for varying roles, but the USAF variant is used almost exclusively by the USAFSC. It is capable of night flight, and can seat up to 13 people. The usual number of crew is two, the pilot and his co-pilot, but in hoist, water and navigational operations the crew is three, with a flight engineer added. Synonymous with the popular image of the Vietnam War, the Huey served with great distinction in all of the US armed forces during the lengthy conflict, and its success cemented hundreds of sales for the manufacturer Bell (more than 5000 served in Southeast Asia in the 1960s). Though originally designed and built in the late 1950s, the Huey still finds itself on the battlefield in its various guises, almost half a century after its conception. Having been in service for almost 50 years, the UH-1N will continue to serve well into the future such is the durability and flexibility of its classic design.

SPECIFICATIONS

Manufacturer:	*Bell Helicopter Textron*
Mission:	*multi-role transport*
Length:	*12.8m (42ft)*
Height:	*4.4m (14ft)*
Rotor Diameter:	*14.6m (48ft)*
Crew:	*3*
Propulsion:	*1 x Lycoming T53-L13B*
Horsepower:	*1100 shaft horsepower*
Maximum Speed:	*204km/h (127mph)*
Cruise Speed:	*185km/h (115mph)*
Vertical Rate of Climb:	*485m/min (1600ft/min)*
Range:	*370km (231 miles)*
Weight:	*2600kg (5800lb)*
Date Deployed:	*1983*
Guns:	*none*
Missiles:	*none*
Systems:	*GPS, winch*

UH-60L BLACK HAWK

The UH-60L Black Hawk is one of the US Army's most recognizable and widely used aircraft. Brought into service towards the end of the 1970s, it is designed as a multi-purpose utility helicopter. In this capacity it is able to transport up to 11 fully armed troops, one 105mm howitzer or many other types of cargo up to a weight of 10,000kg (22,000lb). The Black Hawk has performed admirably in a variety of missions, including air assault, air cavalry and aeromedical evacuations. In addition, modified Black Hawks operate as command and control, electronic warfare and special operations platforms. The UH-60L variant is the workhorse of the US Army, and it has been involved in every operation where US soldiers have been needed. Introduced in 1989, the UH-60L is an improvement on the UH-60A, expanding the lifetime of the aircraft and making it more capable. It is able to utilize the External Supplies Support System (ESSS) to tailor the aircraft to any given mission, be it in an attack support role with Hellfire missiles or as an aerial minelayer, or even in a reconnaissance capacity. It is an extremely reliable and durable aircraft, and as such has become popular with armed forces the world over. The airframe has lent itself to all manner of roles, including the naval Seahawk version.

SPECIFICATIONS

Manufacturer:	*Sikorsky Aircraft*
Mission:	*multi-mission utility*
Length:	*19.5m (64ft)*
Height:	*4.8m (16ft)*
Rotor Diameter:	*16.5m (53ft)*
Crew:	*3*
Propulsion:	*2 x GE T700-701C*
Horsepower:	*3400 shaft horsepower*
Maximum Speed:	*296km/h (184mph)*
Cruise Speed:	*257km/h (160mph)*
Vertical Rate of Climb:	*472m/min (1550 ft/min)*
Range:	*584km (363 miles)*
Weight:	*5224kg (11,516lb)*
Date Deployed:	*1989*
Guns:	*2 x 7.62mm M-60 machine guns*
Missiles:	*Hellfire, FFAR*
Systems:	*ESSS*

V-22 OSPREY

Boeing's revolutionary V-22 Osprey is a utility transport helicopter with a difference, combining the benefits of rotary- and fixed-wing flight. While the traditional helicopter is suitable for many conditions, it lacks the speed or range of traditional airplanes, and the one successful vertical take-off and landing (VTOL) fixed-wing jet aircraft, the Harrier, is vastly expensive to build and maintain. The V-22 Osprey appears to have solved the problem. Designed to take full advantage of a helicopter's versatility and VTOL capability, plus the fixed-wing aircraft's speed and range, the V-22 Osprey will replace the medium-lift helicopters in all of the US armed services. Despite many teething troubles and setbacks, the Osprey is gradually being brought into service and is proving itself to be highly effective. It works by rotating its propellers to a vertical position in order to take off, and then tilts them to a horizontal position for normal flight. It can then tilt the rotors back to a vertical position to land. This allows it to operate from the deck of a ship, in a confined area or on damaged runways in war-torn areas of the world. A similar machine, the BA609 tilt-rotor aircraft, is currently on trial with the USCG. All of the key US helicopter operators look set to take advantage of tilt-rotor technology.

SPECIFICATIONS

Manufacturer:	*The Boeing Company*
Mission:	*utility transport*
Length:	*17.3m (57ft)*
Height:	*6.7m (22ft)*
Rotor Diameter:	*2 x 11.6m (38ft)*
Crew:	*3*
Propulsion:	*2 x Allison T406-AD-400*
Horsepower:	*12,300 shaft horsepower*
Maximum Speed:	*630km/h (390mph)*
Cruise Speed:	*503km/h (313mph)*
Vertical Rate of Climb:	*332m/min (1090ft/min)*
Range:	*954km (515 miles)*
Weight:	*15,032kg (33,140lb)*
Date Deployed:	*2001*
Guns:	*2 x .50in machine guns*
Missiles:	*none*
Systems:	*VTOL Tiltrotor, electronic warfare*

INDEX

Picture Credits

Aviation Photographs International: 9, 34, 142
Aviation Picture Library: 8, 10, 11, 13, 14, 17, 18, 20, 22, 25, 26, 31, 33, 35, 37, 38, 39, 40, 41, 42, 43,
44, 45, 46, 47, 48, 49, 50, 51, 53, 54, 72, 88, 99, 102, 104, 105, 109, 110, 111, 125, 126, 130, 131, 132,
141, 142, 146, 150, 151, 153, 155, 157, 158, 160, 164, 172, 176, 177, 180, 182, 183, 184, 186, 187, 188
BAe Systems: 15, 16, 19, 24, 27, 28, 29, 30, 32, 52, 86
Chinese Defence Today (www.sinodefence.com): 106, 107, 108
Defence Picture Library: 100, 113, 123
Embraer: 12
Eurocopter: 115, 116, 117, 118, 119, 122, 124
Howard Thacker: 161
Mark Wagner@aviationimages.com: 159
Private Collection: 135, 149, 152, 156, 162, 165, 169
Sikorsky: 181
Simon Watson: 136, 137
The Flight Collection@Quadrant: 138, 145
TRH Pictures: 36, 73, 101, 103, 134, 140, 143, 147, 148, 154, 174, 175
US Coast Guard: 178
US Department of Defense: 21, 23, 55, 56, 57, 58, 59, 60, 61, 62, 63, 64, 65, 66, 67, 68, 69, 70, 71, 72,
75, 76, 77, 78, 79, 80, 81, 82, 83, 84, 85, 87, 89, 90, 91, 92, 93, 94, 95, 96, 97, 128, 163, 166, 167, 168,
170, 171, 173, 179, 185
Westland Helicopters: 112, 120, 121, 127
Wingman Aviation: 133, 139